Canada at
WAR

POST OFFICE TELEGRAPHS.

Government Telegram

Subject of Instructions
Special Priority

Office of Origin

GCP

TO { Press Communique
Troopers London

PC 206 11th aaa

Shortly before dawn this

morning Canadian troops of

the First Army (General Horne)

captured MONS

Chief 0955

Canada at WAR

LESLIE F. HANNON / THE CANADIAN ILLUSTRATED LIBRARY

THE CANADIAN ILLUSTRATED LIBRARY
McCLELLAND AND STEWART LIMITED,
ILLUSTRATED BOOKS DIVISION.
150 SIMCOE STREET,
TORONTO 1, ONT., CANADA.

PUBLISHER JACK McCLELLAND
EDITORIAL DIRECTOR PIERRE BERTON
CREATIVE DIRECTOR FRANK NEWFELD
EDITOR LESLIE F. HANNON
ART DIRECTOR HUGH MICHAELSON
ASSISTANT ART DIRECTOR NICK MILTON
PICTURE EDITOR JANE MURDOCH
ASSISTANT EDITOR WALT McDAYTER
EXECUTIVE ASSISTANT ENNIS HALLIDAY

CONTENTS

Foreword

In the first place, this book is not in any way a history. All military histories have a built-in boredom: they must include all the minutiae of every campaign, which battalion was on the right and which on the left, and only soldiers, professional, amateur or armchair, can read them. The histories—and Canada has some excellent ones—are vital to the national record but they seldom touch the imagination of the busy Canadian citizenry or get on to the family bookshelf. Yet the story of Canada at arms is a truly exciting one, with many episodes as thrilling or harrowing (yes, and inspiring) as anything manufactured for television tube or movie screen. My personal interest in the subject was sharpened nearly two decades ago, in the observation car of a C.N.R. train winding through Yellowhead Pass. In that unlikely location I read, in a selection of sober books offered by the porter, that one Lieut. Alexander Robert Dunn, of Toronto (then York), had won the Victoria Cross in the Charge of the Light Brigade at Balaclava, 1854. How come this colonial boy from Upper Canada College took part in the world's most famous feat of arms? Later, I learned that no fewer than 94 Canadians—of a nation supposedly cautious and careful—had won the highest decoration for valour, seven of them in a single day on a foreign field. I discovered that the borders of this huge land had been tested and made secure in war (we even had a mini-army in the Yukon in 1898 to show the line to the Alaskans); and that the march of Canada, of her two races, from frontier colony to modern power, from early adolescence to vigorous maturity, could be followed, in some large measure, on the honour rolls of her military achievement. Politics and punditry have been skirted, or completely avoided, in this book; the keynote is action. Some readers will, I regret, be chagrined that I have omitted reference to the battles of their particular unit — or, indeed, to whole campaigns. Space limitations and personal prejudices are to blame there. Even so, the selection of picture stories offered here states, I submit, that although the Canadians are not a warlike people, they are a fighting people, none better.

The military heritage: the father was Colonel George Burns; the son became General E. L. M. Burns, commander of the 1st Canadian Corps in Italy, later keeper of the peace in the Middle East.

1/ THE BATTLE FOR CANADA

Engraved for Russel's History of England.

The Siege of QUEBEC.

The urge to arms came as naturally as the longing for the open sky of the wide land. It is perhaps the single heritage shared completely by Canadians of the two great racial streams. They fought each other often enough. The two and a half centuries that precede the birth of the nation echo with cannon and the rattle of muskets; the pages of the history of the Canadas glint from the flash of sun on sabre and bayonet, and are streaked with the blood of patriots and brave champions of causes now often forgotten.

We know the day the story begins. Samuel de Champlain, true father of the country, tells it in his own words. He took a party of Indian allies to warn off the ever-aggressive Mohawk. "When I saw them make a move to draw their bows upon us," he wrote, "I took aim with my arquebus and shot straight at one of the three chiefs, and with this shot two fell to the ground . . ." The year was 1609 and the place, the shore of the lake that now bears Champlain's name. That arquebus – a matchlock musket touched off with a smouldering rope wick – set ablaze a guerrilla war, stained by torture, which continued for 80 years and almost drove the first settlers out of the St. Lawrence Valley.

With firearms bought from the Dutch, the warriors of the Five Nations of the Iroquois Confederacy – the Mohawk, Cayuga, Onondaga, Oneida and Seneca, wonderful names ringing with style and power – soon dominated most of the continental north-east, wiping out tribes trading with the French, and eventually carrying the battle to the outposts of Montreal and Three Rivers.

Late one night in the summer of 1689, at the height of a hailstorm, the Indians burst into the village of Lachine to set off an orgy of death and destruction. Men were murdered and scalped on the spot and women and children carried off to be tortured. It was one of the blackest nights of our history. For three months the Iroquois roamed at will in the country around Montreal. At the peak of the terror, when the fate of New France was again in the balance, the great Louis de Buade, Comte de Frontenac, now almost 70, providentially returned as Governor.

The old man knew the name of his real enemy: England. The French had first learned from their 1000-mile raids that the English had taken over from the Dutch on the Hudson River. Now, Thomas Dongan, Governor of New York, was inciting the Iroquois against New France. "The artifices of the English have reached such a point," reported the Marquis de Denonville, "that it would be better if they attacked us openly and burned our settlements instead of instigating the Iroquois against us."

The real battle for Canada was now joined, although from its piratical inception to its Plantagenet finale on the Plains of Abraham it was to span 130 years. The old enemies of Europe found themselves locked in a new kind of struggle in the New World, partly for a king's ransom in furs, partly for a dimly perceived empire the size of many Europes, partly in simple conformity to distant arguments, and partly for the sheer hell of it.

Historians may insist that the long tug-of-war began over our very first settlement, Port Royal (now Annapolis Royal, N.S.) which changed hands many times, beginning in 1614 with the raid by Samuel Argall, operating out of Virginia. But Captain Argall, like several who followed him to the Acadian village, was really just a freebooter out for easy pickings. Quebec was always the heart of New France and we take our date from Champlain's surrender of his colony in 1629 to Sir David Kirke.

It wasn't much of a coup, then. "We were in all 65 souls," Champlain had written the previous year. The Kirke brothers, English Protestants raised in Dieppe, took Quebec from the river in the name of Charles I. The English held it for four years until Charles dealt it back to Louis on the promise the French would pay the dowry owing on Charles' Catholic bride, Henrietta Maria. It was to cost something more than that to retrieve it.

The flinty Frontenac was determined not to sit behind the walls of Quebec and suffer the new English-inspired threat from the south. (To the French, all Americans were "English" until the 19th century.) At first, with the fire-eating Chevalier de Callières, Frontenac planned a

combined sea-and-land attack on New York. France's fatal lack of sea power frustrated that idea and he settled for three overland thrusts. His troops – they could, at a stretch, be called Canada's first invasion force – were mainly Militia drawn from the thin ranks of the colonists, officered partly by regulars who had chosen to remain in New France when their regiments were recalled to Europe.

On snowshoes, in the dead of winter, using the surprise and silence of *la petite guerre* they had so painfully learned from the Iroquois, the Canadians fell upon Schenectady, then a New York frontier outpost, Salmon Falls, north of Boston, and Fort Loyal, the site of the present-day Portland, Maine. Ruthlessly, the raiders burned, killed, and carried off prisoners.

The English-Americans, infuriated, hit back within the year. They sent Sir William Phips up the St. Lawrence to repeat the attack of Kirke 62 years earlier. Phips, commanding from his flagship *Six Friends*, deployed his fleet before the Quebec fortress and sent an envoy to demand surrender. He got this reply from Governor Frontenac: "I will answer your General only with the mouths of my cannon and the shots of my muskets, that he may learn that a man like me is not to be summoned in this fashion."

Phips then pitched 1,500 cannon balls at the wooden stockade and landed 1,300 men just above the mouth of the St. Charles River. The shot did little damage and the Canadians, skirmishing skilfully, penned the invaders into a small beachhead. The impetus of the attack was lost and, after two days, the English backed off in an ignominious retreat that very nearly became a rout.

That dashing commando, Pierre Le Moyne, Sieur d'Iberville, rubbed salt in the English wounds by mopping up all the trading posts on Hudson Bay, and by conquering the English colony of Newfoundland with his "army" of 125 volunteers. He was pleading for a chance to take Boston – and he probably would have made it, too.

The French in the New World had done extremely well but the French at home had, in these same years, the misfortune to collide with the Duke of Marlborough in the complicated nightmare known as the War of the Spanish Succession. When the Treaty of Utrecht wound up the affair, the Canadians had to hand back their gains to the English; they had to hand over Acadia, too, but they managed to retain Cape Breton Island. There, on a marshy promontory, dominating the Cabot Strait entry to the Gulf of St. Lawrence, they immediately began to build a new fortress. They called it Louisbourg.

Conceived in grandeur, behind a ditch 80 feet wide, with walls 30 feet high bristling with 148 guns, Louisbourg was never more than a pretentious eggshell. When the Powers in Europe picked up the war where they had left off, the English-Americans from Massachusetts and Connecticut, convoyed by the Royal Navy, sallied up the coast and beat their way into the fortress with ease. To *their* great anger and frustration, the treaty which ended that phase of the long imperial struggle abroad handed Louisbourg back to the French.

The men of New France now numbered 60,000 against the 1,500,000 of England's restless Thirteen Colonies, but their actions belied their strength. To safeguard the great Canadian hinterland, won principally by the explorations of René de la Salle, they showed the flag vigorously along the Great Lakes and down the Ohio River valley to Louisiana. Fort Rouillé was built on the site of today's Toronto.

In 1753, a gentleman farmer of Virginia, great-grandson of an English squire, was sent to warn the Canadians off the Ohio country. His name was George Washington. That same year, a brilliant young Kentish officer who had helped chase Bonnie Prince Charlie out of Scotland, was heading for high command in the New World. His name was James Wolfe. These two men, on different fields, for different masters, were soon, by force of arms, to create the North America we know.

The opponents in the Seven Years' War read strangely today: on one side – England, Prussia and Hanover; on the other – France, Russia, Austria, Sweden, Saxony and

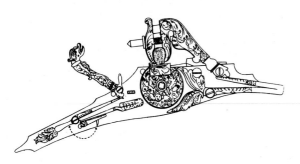

Spain. The grand issues may be foggy now but, for all Canadians, the result is as factual as today. The war began in 1756 and, in the New World for the first two years, the French Canadians walloped the English Americans. The English leaders had still not learned the art of frontier war. Major-General Edward Braddock marched his English red coats and his American blue coats in columns with banners flying against Fort Duquesne – where Pittsburgh now stands – and ran into the waiting Canadians, dispersed in the woods. Hit by a withering fire from guns they couldn't see, Braddock's force broke and ran, leaving behind 977 dead (Braddock himself died later of his wounds). The Canadian loss was 23.

The tide began to turn on June 8, 1758, when Brigadier James Wolfe, frail, 31 years old, led the English ashore at Gabarus Bay, behind Louisbourg. Prime Minister William Pitt (the Elder) had poured 20,000 regulars into the fray. By July 27, every building in ruins, the fortress fell. Wolfe pressed his superior, General Jeffery Amherst, to carry the war immediately to Quebec. "I cannot look coolly upon the bloody inroads of those hell-hounds, the Canadians," Wolfe said. "If nothing further is to be done, I must desire to leave the army."

The hell-hounds, under a 46-year-old general named Montcalm, had just made mincemeat of Commander-in-Chief James Abercromby's overland army of 15,000 at the foot of Lake Champlain. Again, the English columns attacked bravely, frontally, in the European manner; again, the French muskets and cannon, using all possible cover, cut them down. Abercromby lost 2,000 men; Montcalm, 350. "What a day for France!" exulted the Marquis de Montcalm, "What soldiers are ours! I never saw the like." But, with fresh English regulars joining the battle, the weight of numbers told. Fort Frontenac, guarding Lake Ontario at the site of present-day Kingston, was surrendered by its 110 defenders to Colonel John Bradstreet's siege force, 3,000 strong.

The stage was set for conquest. The English were expected to deploy 50,000 men for the task: the last census had shown 15,299 men fit for service in New France. The newly promoted General Wolfe was given an independent command to assault Quebec from the sea, in the wake of Kirke and Phips.

The brave events between June 26, 1759, when the English ships first anchored off the south shore of the Ile d'Orleans, and September 13, when the setting sun on the Plains of Abraham signalled the death of New France, have often been chronicled and have now gathered their especial shroud of legend. If there had been a proper look-out at the cleft of the Anse au Foulon, what then? If Vaudreuil had not been jealous of Montcalm's authority, would the Canadians have been better deployed? Did Montcalm, ordering the charge at 10 o'clock, attack too soon? When both Montcalm and Wolfe were mortally wounded (one painter included both death scenes on the same canvas), did the French break in "horrid, abominable flight . . . ?" It is enough to record here that fine deeds of high courage were wrought in a chivalry which left a legacy of respect and that, on September 18, the white flag was raised over the fortress of Quebec.

The American War of Independence was in the making and the English were soon manning the well-worn Canadian invasion routes against their own erstwhile colonists. Commander-in-Chief George Washington, no longer a loyal subject of the King, reasoned that if the English from their distant bases could subdue the French, his eager rebels could now throw out the English with equal ease and take the whole northern continent.

Benedict Arnold and Ethan Allen moved against Canada at the Quebec border without the courtesy of a declaration of war. Then General Philip Schuyler, on June 27, 1775, marched formally on Montreal, against the thin red line of Sir Guy Carleton's regulars. The Canadians – that is, the native French – must have been intrigued at the prospect of the *les Anglais* fighting *les Anglais*. In the 15 years since the Conquest they could scarcely have become ardent subjects of King George. Fifth columnists from the Thirteen Colonies had rumoured

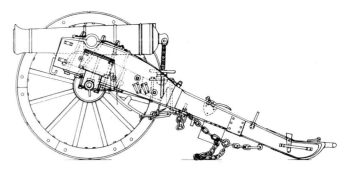

that the English were preparing to ship all the French out of Quebec, in a repetition of the Acadian expulsion.

Carleton had only 1,000 regulars to protect the whole country and when St. Jean fell on November 3 after a long and heroic resistance, he evacuated Montreal and withdrew to Quebec City. On the 13th, the American rebels occupied Montreal and pushed on, under General Richard Montgomery, to invest Quebec.

Montgomery boasted he would have his Christmas dinner in Quebec, or die in the attempt. He missed the dinner but he did keep his date with death – shot by the Canadian Militia as he led his New Yorkers against a barricade at Cape Diamond. Faced with the choice of remaining a separate country under the English or of total absorption by the Americans, the Canadians had made the choice they were to continue to make in the future. Colonel Noel Voyer mustered seven companies of Canadian infantry and a company of artillery to stand alongside the British on the ramparts.

With "Liberty or Death" printed on strips of paper in their caps, the Americans charged in a snowstorm at 4 a.m. on the last day of the year. In the alleys of Lower Town, they were cut down by defenders they seldom saw and, when the muskets were stilled, the snowdrift gently covered the dead and held them until the spring.

Although General Washington thundered that Quebec must be taken, and sent a fresh 2,500 men to reinforce his army, the Americans gave up the siege when the first British relief ship arrived on May 5, 1776. As they fell back in despair and disorder, they could easily have been annihilated by the woods-wise Canadians – now actively hostile – but General Carleton, busy counting heads on the continent, was shrewdly seeking an advantageous peace.

He didn't get it. The Treaty of Paris, 1783, gave the Americans victories in Canada they had not been able to win in the field. The Yankee excursions into Nova Scotia had also failed, but Benjamin Franklin and his diplomatic colleagues actually proposed that *all* Canada be ceded to the United States as a gesture of goodwill from Britain. He did get, though, from an England thoroughly disillusioned with the Americas, intrusive chunks of the Maritimes, Lake Champlain, and the acceptance of the 49th parallel as the western border, thus gathering up without a battle the whole of the great Ohio Valley which had been Canadian for more than a century.

The treaty didn't really take and for the next thirty years British policy in Canada was to prepare to repel the Yankees again. By 1809, the number of regulars on the Canadian frontier totalled 8,000 and the Duke of York had strengthened Halifax to play its historic role as the "Warden of the North." At Kingston, ships of war were gathered to patrol Lake Ontario. A unit of 1,200 men was raised in Upper Canada by Lieut. Governor John Graves Simcoe.

In 1810, the sense of impending drama sharpened with the arrival at centre stage of one of Canada's authentic, if imported, heroes: General Sir Isaac Brock. Born at St. Peter's Port, in the English Channel islands, in the same year as both Napoleon and Wellington, Brock personifies the Canadian martial mystique. He was larger than life: too large for life. He was 6 ft. 2 ins. tall, a big, gay, fair-haired horse-riding man of a courage never plumbed. Only four months after the long-awaited war began, he was dead, sword in hand, an American sniper's bullet in his breast, his face toward the enemy on Queenston Heights, above the Niagara River.

The last great contest for Canada – the War of 1812-14 – had still a long grinding course to follow, much more blood was to be spilled in battles that ranged from Lake Superior to the Atlantic shore, the towns of York and Washington were to burn, but Isaac Brock was already assured his immortality. The soaring 210 ft. column raised on the Queenston escarpment in perpetual warning view of the Americans quickly became more than just a memorial to a hero but the unforgettable souvenir to Canadians of a sovereignty bought in blood.

It was bought, mostly, in British blood. Official military historian C. P. Stacey says, "The chief credit for the

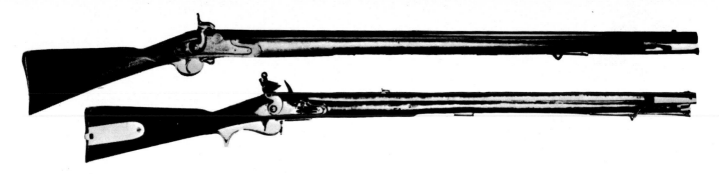

saving of Canada in 1812 is due to British soldiers. It was scientifically defended by men trained for the job. The regulars did more than supply the leadership. They usually did the lion's share of the fighting . . ." Under the peace terms, everybody went back to square one. And Napoleon, who had sparked the whole thing, had just escaped from Elba and was busy setting up the next round.

For more than half-a-century, however, Canada was not dragged into any more of Europe's endless power struggles. There was hardly a year, though, that didn't provide enough threat or excitement to ensure that Canada kept its powder dry and its sentries alert. Minor rebellions flared in both Upper and Lower Canada in 1837 as extremists took to arms against the stiff-necked autocrats entrenched in authority under the newly crowned Victoria.

The Quebec rising, usually said to have been led by Louis Joseph Papineau (who fled to the U.S. before the first shot was fired), was put down by Sir John Colborne's red coats with unnecessary severity; there were few casualties on either side but so many *habitant* villages were put to the torch that Colborne's field commander was dubbed "Old Firebrand."

The Ontario adventure led by William Lyon Mackenzie was close to comic opera. A ragged band with "rifles, old fowling pieces, Indian guns, pikes etc." began a march on Toronto on December 5 from Montgomery's tavern. They fled at the first brush with a patrol under the local Sheriff (so did the Sheriff). When the Torontonians gathered their wits, and some reinforcements, they marched up Yonge Street with two military bands blaring and swept the handful of rebels into the woods. Mackenzie had, like Papineau, slipped away to the States, but two of his lieutenants were hanged for treason and his "General," a Dutchman called Anthony Van Egmond, died in prison.

Those Americans still nursing hopes of absorbing Canada encouraged Mackenzie to shout defiance from Navy Island, in the Niagara River, and loony invasion plans were hatched. At Prescott, on the St. Lawrence,

a mixed bag of Yankees led by a Pole called Nils von Schoultz landed by schooner from Oswego. They were mopped up after desultory scrapping, leaving 160 prisoners. Von Schoultz was hanged at Fort Henry after calling a lawyer to make a will . . . the lawyer was a young comer called John A. Macdonald.

The American dream of annexing the whole continent died hard (if, indeed it *is* entirely dead). Within ten years, James Polk had been elected President on the slogan of "Fifty-four Forty or Fight" – referring to America's Manifest Destiny to control the whole of the Pacific Coast. That particular threat led to Canada strengthening and sharpening the defences across the country as recommended by the Duke of Wellington. Those forts were manned, and our British Enfield rifles well oiled, when the American Civil War in 1861 brought fresh and violent pressure against the border.

That same John A. Macdonald, now risen from the ruck of provincial politicians to become Minister of Militia, tried to get the Active Militia boosted to 50,000 men, but his government was defeated on the issue. The Governor-General of the time fumed about his "parish politicians" and a London alarmed by the anti-British sentiment of the huge armies raised by the Northern States poured an extra 15,000 troops into the colony.

By the spring of 1865, when Robert E. Lee surrendered to Ulysses S. Grant at Appomattox, the Americans had half a million dead to count and no plans to invade anyone. That threat to Canada had passed but another of, luckily, different dimensions immediately materialised. The Fenian Brotherhood, an Irish emigrant organisation inspired by the truly Irish notion that when they had driven the British out of Canada the English would be forced to leave Ireland, was obviously determined to try its luck. The hard core of the Brotherhood was made up of men just discharged from the Union armies.

The decade just passing had seen a new development in the multi-faceted story of Canada at war: with little derring-do available at home, Canadians began to appear

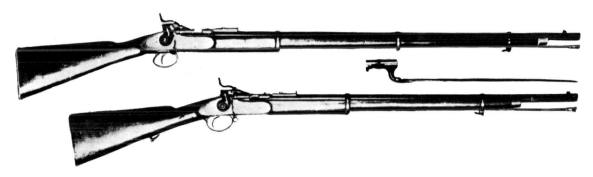

on foreign battlefields. Lieut. Alexander Dunn, of Toronto, had won Canada's first Victoria Cross when he took part in the Charge of the Light Brigade in the Crimea in 1854. Four years later, the 100th Royal Canadian Regiment of Foot fought in the British cause in India. Five hundred Canadians rushed to Italy to fight for the Pope when Garibaldi's legions were on the march to Rome. Those adventuring units were not, however, *officially* Canadian; the 20,000 Militia who turned out to repel the Fenians most definitely were.

In the event, although the Irish had grandiose battle plans that would not have shamed the Carthaginians, only two or three forays were actually attempted. They ended ignominiously but, paradoxically, they played a significant role in convincing the Fathers of Confederation they could stand united and would most probably fall if they remained divided. In 1868 a Fenian thug assassinated D'Arcy McGee, the one "Father" who had insistently warned of the continuing threat from the south, and Sir George Etienne Cartier won an easy passage in the federal Parliament for his Militia Bill.

Canada now had its own volunteer army – on paper, at any rate. The strength of the Militia soon reached 45,000 and it was backed up by a reserve which listed all the rest of the fit adult males in the land.

First blood went to the new force at Eccles Hill, on the Quebec-Vermont border, in the bayonet charge that routed the last of the Fenians on May 25, 1870. But another, graver, task was shaping for the Canadian national army in the West: Louis Riel, 26-year-old leader of the French-speaking Catholic buffalo hunters and squatters on the Red River who had been treated with callous ineptitude by the Federal authorities, declared himself President of the Republic of Manitoba. Rebellion! Or so it was deemed to be in Ottawa and the last British Army regulars remaining in the Dominion – the 60th Rifles – were despatched to quell it. The force, led by Colonel Garnet J. Wolseley, included two battalions of Canadian Militia, one each from Quebec and Ontario.

The British weren't keen to go at all, and after a remarkable trip overland from Lake Superior to Fort Garry, they gave three cheers for the Queen, drank all the whisky they could find in Winnipeg, then set off for the return journey. Riel had fled to the States.

It was, tragically, but the first act of the divisive drama to be staged on the Prairies. When Riel returned from exile in 1885 to lead a second revolt of his *Métis* – now supported by the Indians of Poundmaker and Big Bear – the Canadians of the East reacted with all the mindless muscle of a stripling nation in its eighteenth year. It was their first chance to run a campaign without British help . . . overlooking the fact that the General Officer Commanding, Frederick B. Middleton, was a Britisher as pukka as they come. Middleton met his match in the illiterate Gabriel Dumont, field commander for the paranoic Riel, but when cannon and Gatling gun were brought to bear on hungry men using nails and even stones in their buffalo guns, the final result was never in question.

The last rebellion damped, the Dominion was safe *a mari usque ad mare.* Colonel Wolseley had become a viscount and a field-marshal. General Middleton was granted a knighthood and given a bonus of $20,000. Canadian Colonel W. D. Otter, the saviour of Battleford, went on to become a knight also and Chief of the General Staff. Gabe Dumont became a performer in an American Wild West show. Louis Riel, crazed or sane, was hanged as a traitor to the land he had loved too much. The cost: 105 killed (the forces of the Queen, 70; the rebels, 35); five million dollars.

But that is only what it says in the archives. The true cost of the Canadian Civil War was the reopening of wounds healed since the Conquest, the bitterness reborn in the merciless exercise of the English-speaking Protestant might over the French-speaking Catholic minority. When Prime Minister John A. Macdonald swung in effigy from a Montreal gallows, a shadow was cast on the new nation that, in war as in peace, would not vanish within the present reckoning.

The defence: Frontenac repels the English

Earlier in the year (it was 1690) Sir William Phips had sacked Port Royal; now he sailed from Boston against Quebec. Governor Frontenac had only barrels of stones to block his gates but his cannon scored heavily on the besieging ships. Phips landed 1,300 men who soon withdrew. New France was to stand seventy more years.

A French artist's later impression of the siege of 1690. Did Quebec boast eight spires in her 82nd year? No matter, the 1,000 regulars and the first Militiamen allowed not one invader to put a foot on the rock. Reinforcements under Callières had hurried from Montreal to defend the tiny capital.

It began on Cape Breton. Brigadier Wolfe led his red coats ashore at Louisbourg in a wild surf and, in 49 days, broke into the fortress.

Surprise won Canada. Wolfe — now General Wolfe — landed undetected below Quebec on September 13 and had 4,800 men on the plains of Abraham by daybreak.

The conquest: Wolfe storms the bastions

The Seven Years' War – or Third Silesian War – deserves a bigger page in history: it laid the foundations for the *Pax Britannica*, the empire in India, the modern Germany and, among these happenings, it decided the fate and future of Canada. The year the war started the Canadians, under Louis Joseph Montcalm, stormed the British fort at Oswego (now in New York State), taking 1,600 prisoners and winning control of the Great Lakes. The next year, Montcalm won another victory at Lake Champlain. But in 1759, on the Plains of Abraham, he met his match in General James Wolfe. In one of the greatest of battlefield dramas, both generals perished but it was the British who held the field at sundown.

The French had one last chance. They had been beaten but not destroyed by Wolfe and now the Duc de Lévis attempted, on April 28, 1760, to retake the capital. After the bloody battle of Ste. Foy, the British retired within Quebec until reinforced by sea. Montreal surrendered in the fall and Canada was in British hands.

The Americans invade, 1812-14: the struggle for survival

It was, ostensibly, only a sideshow of the Napoleonic Wars but its intent was clear enough – nothing less than formal conquest. Canada got in first licks by the audacious capture of Detroit with the help of the Shawnees led by Tecumseh, and this was swiftly followed by the stirring victory on Queenston Heights. Reverses came, too – the defeat at Moraviantown, at Fort George, the sacking of Toronto – but success at Stoney Creek, Chateauguay and Lundy's Lane evened scores. The war ended with Canada biting off a large chunk of Maine – which she had to disgorge under the Treaty of Ghent.

The American assault boats — there were actually 13 of them — set out over the Niagara River at Queenston at 3 a.m. on Tuesday, October 13, 1812. One company climbed the 200 ft. escarpment and captured the Canadian gun positions. There they stayed until Major-General Roger Sheaffe, with reinforcements — including Capt. Robert Runchey's Company of Coloured Men, and the York (Toronto) Militia — drove them out at bayonet point. American commander Winfield Scott waved his white handkerchief and the battle was done. Scoreboard: United States — 300 killed or wounded, 958 taken prisoner; Canada — 91 killed or wounded, 21 missing.

Although he was killed in the first unsuccessful charge, the glory of Queenston has always been Isaac Brock's. Commander-in-Chief of the forces in Canada, Brock was in bed at Fort George when the cannonading at Vrooman's Point sent him galloping into action, raising the alarm along the way. Already a hero for his defeat of General Hull at Detroit, Brock had almost personally rallied the country to its defence. Now, in full uniform, sword in hand, ahead of his men, he charged at the invader. A sniper got him.

Governor Col. Guy Carleton, who had served under Wolfe, reviews his troops in Montreal's Place d'Armes before sallying out to seize the American raider Ethan Allan at Longue Pointe in 1775. In the Revolutionary War, President Washington said Congress was "determined on the reduction of Quebec" but his strong army straggled home in rags.

The aggression wasn't always from the south. Frontenac and Callières itched to attack Albany and New York and raided deep into present-day Maine, Virginia, Pennsylvania and New York State. The Marquis de Vaudreuil ordered the capture of Fort Oswego **(below)** in the summer of 1756. Crossing Lake Ontario from Fort Frontenac, they achieved complete surprise.

The ever-present threat from the south

For more than a century, the central problem of Canadian life was the threat of invasion from the swiftly developing colossus to the south. From the first American national attempt to conquer Canada in 1775-76 (when Montreal fell but Quebec stood) to the last Fenian raid of 1870, Canada fought off all attempts – both military and political – to incorporate her in the U.S.A. The fact that we preferred to remain colonial vassals of the cruel and corrupt Crown both disturbed and baffled the Americans. Now-forgotten battles raged between ships-of-the-line on the Great Lakes and off the Atlantic shore. Fifth columnists were active and the Indians were bribed to turn against the British (they didn't). The defended border was sorely dented on several occasions and, if words were bullets, not a Canadian could have survived. Henry Clay boasted that the Kentucky Militia alone could capture Canada but, as the War of 1812 clearly demonstrated, not Kentucky nor the whole republic was equal to the task.

Off Boston, sailors of H.M.S. *Shannon* leapt on to Yankees' *Chesapeake*.

Aiming to sever Canada's lifeline of the St. Lawrence, General James Wilkinson's American army of 8,000 men and 12 gunboats descended the river in 1813. At Cook's Point, 20 miles west of Cornwall, he landed near John Crysler's farm. There he was defeated by 800 men, regulars and Militia, under the dashing leadership of Col. Joseph Morrison.

Veterans' reunion, Toronto, 1859. Survivors of the War of 1812-14, the last American attempt to conquer Canada, meet for an historic photograph.

The 10th Royal Grenadiers and the Queen's Own
Rifles march out of the Toronto Armouries
on March 28, 1885, on their way to crush
the rebellion of the *Métis* in the Nor'west.

In a rare show of initiative, General Middleton
sandbagged the *Northcote* and tried to
enfilade Dumont's defences at Batoche.
He forgot about the ferry cable over the river.

Insurrection in the West: the new nation flexes its muscles

When Louis Riel, a preposterous halfbreed, tried to set
up a republic of the dispossessed in Manitoba in 1870, he
was chased away to the U.S.A. and a price put on his
head. When the very same fellow returned in 1885 and
tried again, in the upper Saskatchewan country, Canada—
with heavy-handed zeal – sent its amateur army against
him. William Van Horne, eager to prove the worth of his
Canadian Pacific Railway, raced 7,982 men to the West—
even where he had no rails yet. It was a Canadian show
but, of course, the officers dined apart from the rank-and-
file and all the proprieties were observed. Gabriel Dumont,
captain of the *Métis* buffalo hunters, observed none of the
proprieties and won at Duck Lake, set a clever ambush at
Fish Creek, and scalped a river gunboat with the Batoche
ferry cable. But, on May 12, while General Middleton
was lunching in his tent, the Midland Militia from Port
Hope and the Grenadiers from Toronto charged without
orders and the Canadian Civil War was over. Riel was
hanged. Canada had yet to learn *O, it is excellent/ to have
a giant's strength, but it is tyrannous/ to use it like a giant.*

Where gaps still existed in the C.P.R. line, the troops marched over lake ice. The main army gathered near Qu'Appelle where many men who had never pulled a trigger were trained.

War correspondents, and artists for the new illustrated papers, now travelled with the troops. Here, the 7th Fusiliers, from London, Ont., are being entertained in Port Arthur.

Cooks and orderlies prepare dinner for the officers' mess during the actions against Riel's forces. A medal was later struck for the victors with Queen Victoria's head in diadem.

At the rebel capital, Batoche, Riel's men were well dug in but short of food and ammunition. Impatient with costly sniping, the Militia finally charged to win a pathetic victory.

Adventures in Africa:
Canada answers the call of Empire

Off to far Egypt to succour brave Gordon in Khartoum: 386 lumberjacks and Indians gathered at Ottawa before departure in 1884.

Voyageurs' task was to get the British expedition through the cataracts of the Nile. They were too late to save General Gordon.

First real glory abroad came in South Africa. Royal Canadian Regiment **(above)** showed great dash at Paardeburg, Feb. 27, 1900.

Canadians assault a *kopje.* "There are no finer or more gallant troops in all the world," said General Sir Horace Smith-Dorrien.

The field hospital at Paardeburg Drift received 130 Canadian casualties. A total of 7,368 Canadians served in South Africa.

The enormous homeland now secure – as long as the Yankees didn't get any more ideas – Canada was ready to begin an entirely new chapter. The action lay abroad, in the remote lands still under good Queen Victoria's sceptre. Everyone stirred to Kipling: *Then it's Tommy this, an' Tommy that, / An' Tommy, 'ows your soul? / But it's 'Thin red line of 'eroes,' / When the drums begin to roll.*

The eager response to Lord Wolseley's request for *voyageurs* for his Nile campaign and the spirit and dash of the Royal Canadian Regiment in the South African War (*pictures*, pages 26-27) showed the temper of the times. Some farmers' sons from the West joined up for six months to help steer the British through the Nile rapids and they hadn't been in a boat in their lives. Wolseley reached Khartoum too late to save General "Chinese" Gordon from the hordes of the Mahdi and the brutal murder on the steps of the British Residency shocked loyalists everywhere; a large number of Canadians plagued the War Office in London with offers of service. Sir Charles Tupper urged Sir John A. Macdonald to offer a fighting unit (as Australia had already done). The Prime Minister refused sourly: "The Suez Canal is nothing to us..."

When the pressure was resumed to answer the call of Empire in South Africa in 1899, Prime Minister Wilfrid Laurier gave a different answer. Although worried by some Quebec opinion that sensed a plot in English-speaking endeavours anywhere, he sanctioned the despatch of several Canadian contingents to help subdue the Boer Republics. In the nation's first officially recognised intervention abroad, 7,368 men served with the British forces, including a mounted rifles unit raised and paid for by the C.P.R. magnate, Donald Smith, now Lord Strathcona and Mount Royal, the High Commissioner for Canada in London. Dubbed Lord Strathcona's Horse,

it was led by the famed Col. Sam Steele of the Mounties.

The Canadians began to build their overseas reputation for raw courage. General Sir Redvers Buller said of Lord Strathcona's Horse that he had never been served by "a nobler, braver or more serviceable body of men"; a sergeant in that unit won the Victoria Cross. At Leliefontien, one astonishing day, three Canadians – all former Militiamen – won the highest decoration in a single action; one of them, Lieutenant R. E. W. Turner, survived to command a famed Canadian division in the Great War.

The Canadians also launched their reputation for breezy disregard of rank and entrenched privilege. *Punch* soon carried the cartoon in which a Canadian officer is instructing his men: "And now, boys, we are to be inspected by an English general. And while he is here, be careful not to call me 'Alf'."

Rather than truckling to England's demands, Laurier had pointed the road ahead for Canada's independent action: "Canada shall be at liberty to act or not to act . . . she shall reserve for herself the right to judge whether or not there is cause for her to act." That time had indeed come, as Britain was soon to withdraw the last vestiges of her power from Canadian soil. The last field unit of the British Army in Canada (the 60th Rifles) had left for home after the Red River Rebellion and only the naval garrisons at Esquimalt and Halifax remained. The swelling strength, and the threatening demeanour, of the Triple Alliance powers in Europe called the Navy back to home waters and Canada took over the dockyards. Now, after a tenure of 157 years, during which they had conquered the land and defended it against all threat, the British sailed away from Halifax to the haunting skirl of the pipes. They were gone forever, and the Canadians, from now on, could fight their own battles.

Inset When the Dominion was secure from sea unto sea, Canadians began to fight abroad — beginning in the Boer rebellion, South Africa.

At right Canadian infantry of the 22nd Battalion attacking near Arras, France – detail from the painting by Lieut. Alfred Bastien.

2/THE GREAT WAR

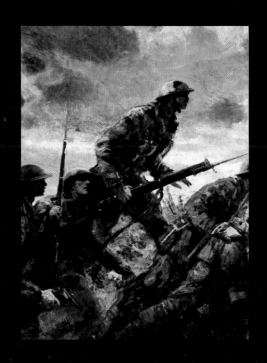

In late July 1914, when war was inevitable and imminent in Europe, the Prime Minister of Canada, Sir Robert Laird Borden, was enjoying a planned month's holiday golfing and bathing at the Muskoka lakes. When the German Army had already seized hapless Luxembourg and sent cavalry patrols into France, the Governor-General, Field-Marshal H.R.H. the Duke of Connaught, was on vacation at Banff, half a continent away from the command post of the nation. Parliament was not sitting and the rest of the hard-working population of eight millions was eager to join in the traditional summer holiday.

Ill-prepared as Canada was, a few war horses were snorting in their straw. In Ottawa, furious at what he considered Britain's delay in declaring war, Colonel Sam Hughes, the megalomaniac provincial publisher who held the portfolio of Militia and National Defence, ordered the Union Jack lowered at his office. "By God!" he shouted, "I don't want to be a Britisher under such conditions." At one minute past midnight on August 5, the British did go to war, carrying with them the Dominion of Canada and the rest of the Empire upon which the sun had never set.

When the awful battle was over, four years and three months and six days later, England stood bled and exhausted, falling back from her imperial zenith. But the Canadians – as though it had been some interminable Iroquois manhood ritual – survived the test of fire, waxed stronger, and advanced with undreamed-of speed toward the responsibility of nationhood and, more importantly, toward a realisation of their unique identity.

In 1914, Canada went to war without a voice of her own, with a regular army of 3,110 souls and 684 horses, a navy of just 300 men, and an air force consisting of two canvas planes still packed in crates. Only 12 regular officers had completed staff college courses. It is easy to understand the opinion of a German general, writing a military appreciation for Supreme Command in Berlin, that the colonial Canadians could play no significant part in any European war. The Militia, enthusiastic amateurs given to foppish uniforms and quadrilles, were described by Colonel W. Hamilton Merritt, of the Canadian Governor-General's Horse Guards, recently returned from the sharp realities of the South African War, as part of "the most expensive and ineffective military system of any civilised community in the world." Most Militiamen spent four days a year in camp.

In 1918, incredibly, Canada stood at the spearhead of the thrust into the enemy-held territory with her own full Corps of 100,000 fighting men under Canadian generals, with a combat reputation second to none, and, in 1919, walked forward to put her own signature on the Treaty of Versailles. In that era – it already seems as distant as the Crusades – the great majority of Canadians were glad to fight for gallant Belgium and mother England. The greatest French Canadian of all time, Wilfrid Laurier, said immediately: "There is in Canada but one mind and one heart . . . today we realise that Great Britain is at war and that Canada is at war also." (Even through the worst of the conscription riots that were to come in 1918 it was Laurier, and not isolationist Henri Bourassa, who spoke veritably for Quebec.)

When the call went out, recruiting offices from Halifax to Victoria were flooded with men – it was patriotism, all right; a private's pay was only a dollar a day – and special trains raced the first 32,665 accepted volunteers through cheering crowds to Valcartier, a tent camp literally thrown up beside the Jacques Cartier River, near Quebec City. The authorities, who had offered Britain on August 10 a contingent of 25,000, had far more men than they needed. Colonel Hughes (he was soon to promote himself to General) crowed with delight. He strutted up the Valcartier lines in sword and plumed hat; on grand occasions he mounted a charger. In the streets of Montreal, Canadians of both races linked arms and sang *La Marsellaise* and *Rule Britannia*.

Within two months the First Division, Canadian Expeditionary Force, was heading across the Atlantic, escorted by ten warships. In its fervid haste, the convoy left behind on the Quebec dock-side, 800 horses and 5,000 tons of ammunition and equipment. Inevitably, as with all armies in all eras, it was a case of "hurry up and wait." On reaching England, the basically-untrained Canadians had to endure a long cold winter in the mud and drizzle of the Salisbury Plain tent camp.

Sentry: 'Alt, who goes there?
Reply: Scots Guards.
Sentry: Pass, Scots Guards.

Sentry: 'Alt, who goes there?
Reply: The Buffs.
Sentry: Pass, the Buffs.

Sentry; 'Alt, who goes there?
Reply: Mind your own God-damn business!
Sentry: Pass, Canadians.

By the time the First Division was deemed ready for the front line, in the spring of 1915, every man was razor-keen. Nothing, they told each other, could be worse than Salisbury. In the 43 months that lay ahead, they – and the 400,000 other Canadians who followed them overseas – were to find out just how tragically wrong that assessment was.

The following pages record the costly battle honours: Ypres, where the Canadians stemmed the onrushing enemy after poison-gas was released; the senseless savagery of Festubert and Mount Sorrel; the killing ground of the Somme in 1916; the heart-lifting victory of Vimy Ridge; the bloody bog of Passchendaele; the whirling aerial dogfights dominated by young Dominion pilots; the heroic cavalry charge where a boy called Gordon Muriel Flowerdew, from Duck Lake, Sask., won the Victoria Cross (and died in the winning); and, finally, the advance of the Hundred Days which ended as Lieutenant-General Sir Arthur Currie, the ex-schoolteacher from Napperton, Ont., formally occupied Mons at 11 a.m. on November 11, 1918. That was exactly where the Empire's war on the Western Front had begun.

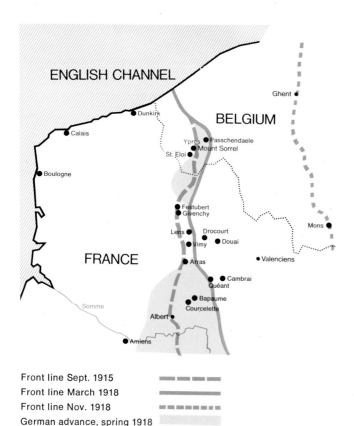

ENGLISH CHANNEL

Ghent

BELGIUM

Dunkirk

Calais

Ypres ● Passchendaele
● Mount Sorrel
St. Eloi ●

Boulogne

Festubert
Givenchy

Mons

Lens ● Drocourt
● Vimy ● Douai

FRANCE

● Arras

● Valenciens

● Cambrai
Quéant

● Bapaume
Courcelette

Somme

Albert ●

● Amiens

Front line Sept. 1915

Front line March 1918

Front line Nov. 1918

German advance, spring 1918

There were, however, other campaigns that have been nearly, or totally, forgotten in the swift rush of years. Canadians, for instance, were locked in fierce battle with the Communists (they called them the "Bolshies" then) on the Dvina River, south of Archangel, in northern Russia, when Armistice Day was being celebrated in other parts. More than 500 Canadians – mostly the 16th Field Artillery Brigade – were sent from Scotland to join British and American troops in a futile attempt to bolster the anti-Communist White Russians. They won a fistful of medals and the last of them didn't get back to Britain until the fall of 1919. Another, much bigger, Canadian force was sent on the same forlorn quest to Siberia, on Russia's eastern flank. It is wryly amusing to recall the Canadian Prime Minister's explanation for this political intervention. "Intimate relations with that rapidly developing country," Sir Robert Borden said, "will be a great advantage to Canada in the future."

An adventure into the Caucasus in the summer of 1918, with the idea of protecting the Baku oilfields from the Turkish enemy, was shared with gusto by 15 Canadian officers and 26 non-commissioned officers. It reads like an adventure serial out of *Boys' Own Paper* – and well it might, as the commanding officer was Major-General L. C. Dunsterville, the original "Stalky" of Rudyard Kipling's tales. In scenes of sheer chaos, amid demoralized Russians, terrified Armenians and murderous Jangali tribesmen, the Canadians tried to rally a ragtag army to defend the oilfields. On the night of September 14, the British force was evacuated by ship down the Caspian Sea.

Some Canadians spent their war on islands in the sun. At the outbreak, in what could unkindly be called a perfect demonstration of military logic, Canada's only trained infantry battalion, the Royal Canadian Regiment, was shipped off to Bermuda for garrison duty. The following year, Canadian artillery was sent south to guard St. Lucia, in the Windward Isles. On Lemnos, in the Mediterranean, Canadian hospital units cared for casualties from the ill-fated Gallipoli campaign and themselves became casualties when a most unexpected foe – frostbite – hit the area. Four hundred cases were admitted in one week.

In western Europe, a small army of Canadians toiled in forestry, railway and tunneling companies. No fewer than 22,094 lumbermen were overseas by 1918, making good the losses in imports caused by the German submarine attacks. Apart from setting records for daily output of sawn timber, they hacked out more than 100 airfields for the British and French air forces. The tunnelers had one of the war's hardest and most dangerous jobs as they burrowed beneath the enemy trenches to lay explosives. At Mount Sorrel, in June 1916, the 2nd Canadian Tunneling Company was trapped while underground by an enemy counterattack and suffered 96 casualties. The Canadian railway battalions – mostly men past normal military age – were responsible for laying and maintaining most of the light railway network supplying the static front-line positions. In the last 20 months of the war, they put down – often under shellfire – 1,169 miles of standard-guage line and 1,404 miles of tramway.

When General Sir Edmund Allenby, pursuing the Turks in Palestine with the help of Lawrence of Arabia, realised the enemy would probably destroy the rail bridges of the Yarmuk Valley, he asked for Canadian help. The story of how Sir William Van Horne and his C.P.R. engineers had got the troops through the Canadian Shield in 1885 – even when there were no rails – had been carefully filed in military archives. A company of 256 men was raised and, in October 1918, the Turks having duly blown the bridges, the Canadians set to work in one of the world's most unpleasant spots. A thousand feet below sea level, they lived with man-eating mosquitoes, six-inch centipedes, poisonous spiders and scorpions. But, in 19 days, they opened the rail to Damascus.

Although Newfoundland was, of course, at this time a separate colony of Britain's (her oldest, in fact), mainland Canadians observed the island's inspiring war record with a special pride, and even more anguish. The Newfoundland Regiment was cut to pieces at Beaumont Hamel, on the Somme, on the fateful morning of July 1, 1916. The attacking islanders bunched at the few gaps cut in the enemy wire and, within an hour, the German machine-gunners had mown down 684, half of whom died. Again, in the spring of 1917, the Regiment suffered grievously in a mismanaged attack at Monchy-le-Preux. Canada, and the rest of the Empire, raised a cheer when a 17-year-old from Middle Arm named Tom Ricketts was awarded the Victoria Cross in the fighting near Courtrai. No-one seems to have been horrified at the spectacle of a mere boy on the battlefield – Ricketts had enlisted at 15 and had been previously wounded.

All these events are dimmed by the merciful cloak of time – all except one: Vimy. The name of this rolling ridge between the towns of Arras and Lens in northern France is remembered less in the fine words on the marble memorial Canada placed on the crest than in the unwritten record of the country's subtle transformation from brash, brave adolescence to sober, painful maturity.

As a battle, it was not the greatest. It was part of a huge assault by two British armies that, in total, ended in the usual stalemate. Canadians elsewhere fought longer, tougher and more costly actions. But, at Vimy, on Easter Monday 1917, the Canadian Corps – all four divisions – attacked together and triumphed together. It was the first clear-cut national military success abroad, won with dash and determination in a sleet storm. It resulted in the capture of more ground, more guns, more prisoners than any previous British offensive on the Western Front. Four Canadians won the Victoria Cross at Vimy and Major-General Currie, who led the First Division, won a personal knighthood from King George V.

Three years earlier, Currie had been just an unknown Militiaman, an amateur "Saturday night soldier." Now, he was promoted Lieutenant-General and given command of the Corps. His rise to power and leadership from lowly beginnings can serve as an allegory of the fundamental change Canada as a nation underwent in what men called The Great War.

Down a snowy street to a far-off war

From a hundred towns like Fernie, B.C., ordinary Canadian citizens formed ragged ranks and set off with high purpose, never considering, with God and the Royal Navy on their side, the sun could ever set on the greatest empire the world had ever known. More than 600,000 marched off into the Expeditionary Force and nearly half of them were British immigrants. Small boys, as always, ran alongside the columns, wishing they were old enough to go. Before it was over over there, some of them were. And some of them were dead.

OFF TO THE FRONT.
DEPARTURE OF THE THIRD
CONTINGENT FROM FERNIE. B.C.
ON FEB: 28th 1915.

Myths sustain war. One of the most durable in our martial history is that the first Canadians in action in the Great War were the infantry of the First Division who so gallantly (and surprisingly, considering how green they were) stemmed the German breakthrough before the Belgian town of Ypres, in April 1915, when the enemy used poison gas as a terror weapon.

It does not detract from that heroic performance to put it down clearly that another unit, 1,000 strong, Princess Patricia's Canadian Light Infantry, was fighting in the front line while the First Division was still training in England. The "Princess Pats" were raised practically overnight in Ottawa in August 1914 by Captain A. H. Gault, a Montreal veteran of the South African War who contributed $100,000 to the cost of the battalion. They were named for the daughter of the Governor-General.

Detached from the main body of Canadians, the P.P.C.L.I. landed in France in December 1914 with the British 27th Division. They saw action near St. Eloi, and at Polygon Wood where they suffered 80 casualties. Then they were drawn into the same vital, defensive battle at Ypres where their countrymen earned such high praise. Through the next half-century, the "Pats" were to become the best-known unit in the Canadian armed forces.

The First Division actually missed the first gas cloud; it rolled across the 45th Algerian Division, on the Canadian left. The French native troops, still wearing the red baggy trousers of colonial dress, fled and opened a huge gap in the line. Two days later, while they were damming the flood of enemy troops pouring through toward Ypres, the Canadian forward companies were themselves under gas attack. Makeshift gasmasks (a strip of cotton to be wetted and tied over the nose and mouth) were of little protection against the choking chlorine. The Canadians made several withdrawals but eventually stabilized the line.

The First Division was withdrawn after five days of almost continuous, often hand-to-hand, fighting. The Germans had cut the Allied bulge in half but Ypres still stood, battered but defiant. And that was victory.

Lieut. Hugh Niven rallies the "Princess Pats"
at Frezenberg, in the battle for Ypres.
Ordered to withdraw, he refused because he
didn't have enough men to carry the wounded.

In the trenches

In the front line, Canadians snatch rest in simple dugouts that provided some cover from shell splinters. At times, between barrages, a man could hear his German or Austrian lookalike talking just a few murderous yards away. The routine tour of duty in the line was four days. It could seem like eternity.

To young men from the wide prairies and the limitless north woods, the claustrophobia of trench life was almost as bad as the enemy's bullets. In ditches dug from the English Channel to Switzerland, the simple soldiers on both sides fought mud, lice, homesickness, the despair of dirty socks and, every so often, with blind ferocity and little malice, the men who waited and watched only a few yards away.

After an attack, there often wasn't even a trench – just the simple shelter of the shell holes. At night, this new front line would be linked by trenches, duck-boards laid, dugouts constructed for command posts, and someone would put up a sign, "Paradise Alley" or "Yonge Street."

Once, a German held a toy horse above his parapet and a Canadian sniper instantly clipped it. A few minutes later, the horse appeared again, bandaged across the rump. Another time, a sign was hoisted: "Stop Firing! We were at the Somme too."

Moving across a nightmare land, blasted of every blade of grass, Canadian soldiers carry trench supplies into the front line.

The 16th Machine-gunners hold a temporary line in November 1917 in shell holes remaining from the attack. In the trenches of the Western Front, the great aims of the generals were lost to view. Each man could only lunge at the next hump in the ground; a knoll a mile away was as unattainable as Mount Everest.

Wounded men and prisoners came back over the same route, all equally vulnerable if the guns ranged on the communication lines.

The soldier

For long months at a stretch, when the line wavered back and forth only a few yards, the Canadian soldier adapted to the curious unrealities of life under only-occasional fire. After his unit's four-day stint in the front line, he returned along the zigzag communications trenches to the reserve positions where, with only the warning of sudden thunder, long-range guns could drop death in his lap. It was a twilight existence that seemed to produce poets and cynics. One moment a man could be writing a love-letter to his girl in High River; the next, he was just another name to be chiselled into the village cenotaph.

Back home, they would have complained if the bathroom was untidy; up front, a water-filled shell hole was a Roman pool. Shaving was *de rigueur* in the Canadian Expeditionary Force but, in these conditions, even the Colonel had to put up with dirty boots.

It was indeed *A Long, Long Way to Tipperary*
– or could the tune be *Alouette*? A fiddle,
even the humble harmonica, were prized
beyond rubies among men who knew the days
were dwindling before the next big push.

Smiling Canadian drinking hot coffee *(at
right)* has just been wounded in the fierce
fighting for Hill 70 in the mid-summer of
1917. The enemy was 100 yards away when
this photograph was being taken.

Keeping his steel helmet (they called it a
"tin hat") firmly in place, this Canadian
infantryman takes a tub – and just manages
to "stay decent" for the snapshot. His pal
seems unwilling to play the role of valet.

The cook kept his kitchen as close to the
action as possible. When his company was
in the line it was his sacred duty to
get one hot meal a day forward – usually
carried in tin "dixies" by a "fatigue" party.

The storming of Courcelette

". . . The Canadians entered the Somme battle where they played a part of such distinction that thenceforward they were marked out as storm troops and for the remainder of the war they were brought along to head the assault in one great battle after another." The praise came from the British Prime Minister, David Lloyd George, and was earned mainly by the Second Division, led by Major-General R. E. W. Turner, v.c., which attacked and took the village of Courcelette on September 15, 1916. In this action, tanks were first used in warfare and, although the ground was unsuitable, the machines cranky, the tactics hopelessly inept, the 3-m.p.h. 28-ton behemoths still demonstrated that here, at last, was the new idea that could pierce the Western Front and win the war. Hardened soldiers of General Fritz von Below's First Army surrendered in terror to Canadian infantrymen, who seemed to work in instinctive co-operation with the few tanks that made it to the battle line. But the High Command did not grasp the true promise of the tank, properly used. Lieutenant-General Sir Julian Byng, commander of the Canadian Corps at that time (and later to be Governor-General), wrote them off: "They are a useful accessory to the infantry, nothing more."

The Somme remains a name to make men shudder. In five months in that valley in Picardy, the Allies suffered 623,907 casualties. The British lost 57,000 men in one awful morning—their worst defeat since the Battle of Hastings.

Brig. R. Brutinel's machine-gunners in their armoured cars became one of our crack units.

Returning after the fall of Courcelette, Canadians – some wearing trophy helmets – raise a cheer. Regina, Kenora, Sudbury, these were the names they gave to the fortified German trenches in the Somme Valley which cost Canada dearly. The British Fourth Army had attacked on a ten-mile front in the fall of 1916 and here two new ideas in war were tried: the tank and the creeping barrage. The Canadian attack prospered at a total cost of 24,029 casualties but, eventually, the whole assault ran down short of the objective, the town of Bapaume, only a few miles up the Roman road from Albert. The Germans suffered so badly, too, that the commanding General Erich Ludendorff advocated unrestricted submarine warfare to "save the men from a second Somme."

The preparatory barrage (983 guns) at Vimy hammered the ridge for two weeks. Then the Canadians dashed forward, at dawn, in snow and freezing rain.

Just minutes after the capture of a redoubt on Vimy.

Two officers and 75 men surrendered to three Canadians. Prisoners totalled 4,000.

Vimy — the ridge that lives in memory

Still, each summer, a few greying men walk slowly up the steps that now lead to the memorial crowning Vimy Ridge, a seven-mile-long escarpment in the ancient French kingdom of Artois. They are Canadians, in their 70s now, who have returned for a second and last look at the ridge which they rushed and won on Easter Monday, 1917. It was the first time that the Canadian Corps had attacked as a national unit and the rousing victory – the biggest single advance on the Western Front up to that time – soon came to be celebrated as a national coming-of-age. Tested in the fire, the soldiers of the young nation proved at Vimy and in many other battles, that, when intelligently led, they had lost none of the fighting spirit that had always distinguished their frontier ancestors. Foresight helped, too – the gunners lobbed thousands of poison-gas shells into the German rear and killed all the enemy's transport horses.

Opposite: War artist W. B. Wollen depicts capture of a German trench at Vimy. In hand-to-hand fighting, four Victoria Crosses were won.

Mud stopped the tanks, but not the men

Eight of the earliest 28-ton tanks, each with a crew of seven, trundled forward with Major-General H. E. Burstall's Second Division in the attack on Thelus, a battered village on the forward slope of Vimy Ridge.

The sticky mud of Artois, ploughed and harrowed by countless shells, was too much for the 105 h.p. Daimler engines which, at best, could manage 3.7 m.p.h. Once they "bellied down" they were sitting ducks for enemy artillery. But the Canadians swept on, sometimes surprising the enemy still sheltering deep underground from the shells which "poured over our heads like water."

This panorama of the advance at Vimy shows that war for the "foot-slogger" was only seldom the heroic charge beloved of the war artist and novelist. It was bitterly cold that morning in 1917 but the wind was blowing the sleet into the faces of the waiting enemy. Every move had been rehearsed in detail.

The victory was hailed as Canada's Easter
gift to France but the cost was paid in grieving
homes across the Dominion. When cavalry
tried to exploit the gains towards Willerval,
they were cut down by machine-guns.

Probing on to the plain beyond Vimy, a Canadian
brigadier in this "whippet" tank was shelled
moments after this photograph was taken.
The battle ended with the assault on The Pimple
by the 10th Brigade. Then the Canadians
could look down on the suburbs of Lens where
another, even more violent, battle loomed.

It was through this sea of mud, where men weeping with frustration sank to their thighs, that Australians, New Zealanders and then Canadians advanced to Passchendaele. Once, this Belgian land had been beneath the North Sea and when shelling destroyed the drainage ditches, it began to seek the ocean once more.

The Fourth German Army had built five rows of concrete pillboxes, packed with machine-guns that could sweep a murderous hail across the flatlands.

Canadian pioneers construct a pathway over the mire to ease the evacuation of wounded. In the appalling conditions, as many as 12 men had been needed to carry back one stretcher case. A British "brass-hat," seeing the awful battle-field for the first time, cried out: "Good God! Did we really send men to fight in that?"

The battle that should not have happened

Passchendaele comes blithely off the tongue, but it lies most bitterly on the memory of Canada and the other Empire countries whose soldiers perished in their thousands in its bogs and ditches in the fall of 1917. In retrospect, it is almost beyond belief that, after the agonising lessons of the Somme and earlier battles, responsible leaders of men could have insisted (and they did *insist*) on carrying out the operation and, when the attack quickly slumped into the usual pattern of mass-death, in pursuing it for four months.

To Canadians of the First and Second Divisions fell the dubious honour, on November 6, of actually capturing the pathetic ruins of the crossroads village and its neighbouring heights. The 27th Battalion was first into Passchendaele, sparked by the heroism of Private J. P. Robertson who was awarded a Victoria Cross. Robertson did not live to enjoy the dusk; nor did 734 other Canadians who laid down their lives that day (1,504 were wounded).

The offensive gained 4½ miles of mud, which the Germans soon took back again. Winston Churchill called it "a forlorn expenditure of valour and life without equal in futility." Lloyd George, who blamed the "stubborn egotism" of his own Commander-in-Chief, later called it an "insane enterprise." Who would argue?

The last heroic hours of the cavalry

The gallant charge of Lord Strathcona's Horse at Moreuil Wood on March 30, 1918, held for posterity in Sir Alfred Munnings' fine painting, briefly revived memories of the Six Hundred at Balaclava sixty years earlier. But the introduction first of the machine-gun and then of the tank had long since made it clear – except to an obdurate coterie of senior commanders – that the day was done for the dashing cavalry.

The Strathcona squadron, led by Lieut. G. M. Flowerdew *(below),* swept at the gallop, sabres glinting, through the ash trees of the mile-long wood at the startled German infantry attacking Amiens. Mortally wounded, Flowerdew became the third Canadian cavalry subaltern to receive the Victoria Cross.

The Fort Garry Horse and the Royal Canadian Dragoons – under the English commander of the Canadian Cavalry Brigade, Brigadier the Rt. Hon. J. E. B. Seely – were also in action that day in the adjoining Rifle Wood.

The last Canadian action on horseback took place at Le Cateau, during the final advance to Mons. It was, fittingly, a rousing good show: galloping eight miles against dug-in infantry and machine-guns, they rounded up 400 prisoners.

"There's but one task for a

ILLUSTRATED
SUPPLEMENT

The S

VOL. X., No. 37.

MONTREAL, CANA

Who stands if freedom fall

THE LARGEST WHITE CITY EVER PITCHED IN CANADA IN WAR TIME—The above picture show
have volunteered for active service at the front.   This division is three-quarters of a mile in length by ove

on of the wonderful city of tents at Valcartier, now the home of over 30,000 Canadian infantrymen who
le in width.   The total area however, of this extraordinary camp embraces a circumference of ten miles.

The call to arms . . .
and the call for cash

The posters of the Great War evoke a simple unsophisticated land where you could punch first and apologize (perhaps) later: "Dad's on the Line busy fighting, What are **you** doing?" The early recruiting campaigns for the volunteer army were bedevilled by spill-over pacifism and isolationism from the non-combatant U.S.A. where Henry Ford, Woodrow Wilson and the Secretary of State William Jennings Bryan were against the war. Bryan spoke for them all: "If the dogs of war have got to fight it out in Europe, let us avoid hydrophobia at home." Two years of mounting ship losses to German submarines changed

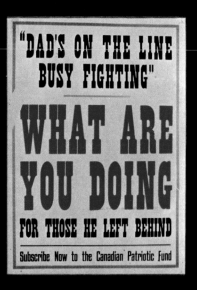

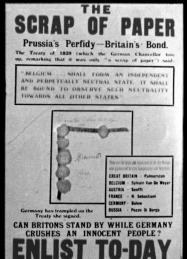

G-Bye Mary

THE PATRIOTIC FUND WILL CARE FOR YOU"

HOW MUCH WILL YOU GIVE

CANADIAN GRENADIER GUARDS

245th Overseas Battalion

Lt.-Col. C. C. BALLANTYNE
OFFICER COMMANDING

"FALL IN THE GUARDS"

"THE CALL FOR MEN of COURAGE"

NOW RECRUITING

RECRUITING DEPOTS:
Canadian Grenadier Guards' Armoury, Fletcher's Field, Montreal
Windsor Arcade Building   140 Peel St., Montreal
Witness Building   Cor. Craig and St. Peter Sts., Montreal

IF YOU CANNOT JOIN HIM

YOU SHOULD HELP HER

CANADIAN PATRIOTIC OFFICE

RIEN À FAIRE — sans L'EMPRUNT DE LA VICTOIRE

APPLY TO POST OFFICES, BANKS, RAILWAY OFFICES AND STORES FOR

THRIFT STAMPS

NATIONAL SAVING

WE LICKED THEM AT THE FRONT

YOU LICK THEM AT THE BACK

HUN OR HOME?

BUY MORE LIBERTY BONDS

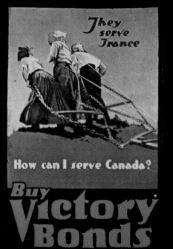

They serve France

How can I serve Canada?

Buy Victory Bonds

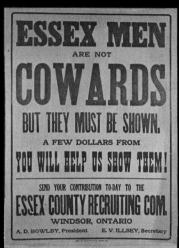

ESSEX MEN ARE NOT COWARDS

BUT THEY MUST BE SHOWN.

A FEW DOLLARS FROM YOU WILL HELP US SHOW THEM!

SEND YOUR CONTRIBUTION TO-DAY TO THE

ESSEX COUNTY RECRUITING COM.

WINDSOR, ONTARIO

A. D. BOWLBY, President   E. V. ILLSEY, Secretary

The young nation rallies behind the fighting men abroad

As the war of attrition ground on in Europe, several of the Allied countries—including Britain itself—mopped up the pool of volunteers and had to turn to conscription. It was a particularly ugly word in Canada and a troubled Prime Minister Borden called an election in 1917 to get national approval for his Military Service Bill. During the electioneering, Canada got a taste of war when two munitions ships blew up in Halifax harbour, killing 1,630 persons. Borden's Union Government won handsomely, but in Quebec could take only three seats out of 65. Bourassa's supporters rioted in Quebec City and Montreal but, all across the land, women exchanged aprons for cover-alls and released men from farms and factories.

Steam thresher held no terrors for these ladylike workers.

Lower left: A Toronto shell factory in full blast, but Canada bought most supplies in the U.K. — to the tune of $252,567,942.03.

Lower right: Stanley Turner painted this homefront scene, complete with glamorous heroes, at Davisville Ave., Toronto.

The new cavalry of the skies

The unique romance of the war in the air, 1914-18, is, perversely, still inspiring after half a century. Death came just as finally, and probably sooner, to the young pilots of the Royal Flying Corps and the Royal Naval Air Service but the mundane world treasures the legends of the devil-may-care flyers who, like jousting knights of another time, threw their flimsy planes across the sky at an equally chivalrous and spirited enemy. At first, the pilots fought with revolvers, rifles and hand grenades. Frenchman Roland Garros then lashed a machine-gun

Canada's great aces: W. A. Bishop, top Allied scorer (72 kills) . . . W. G. Barker *(right)* with Prince of Wales . . . Raymond Collishaw: his bag totalled 60.

All-Canadian No. 203 Squadron, R.A.F., was led by Collishaw *(standing, sixth from left)* still wearing his original naval uniform. With no air force of their own, about 4,000 Canadian servicemen abroad transferred into Britain's air services; others went to England at their own expense and joined up.

on his plane and turned it into a flying gun, shot down five German aircraft and became the first *as de l'aviation* (giving the English-speaking world the familiar "ace").

Adventurous Canadians, many of them frustrated cavalrymen, flocked to the new combat arm. When the air units amalgamated into the Royal Air Force in 1917, about one-quarter of the fighting strength was Canadian. They posted a truly remarkable record. Ten of the 27 leading aces in the R.A.F. were Canadians, and they included two out of the top five scorers of the whole war. Dominion airmen were awarded more than 800 decorations, including three Victoria Crosses.

The "Flying Circus" of German Capt. Manfred von Richthofen (his *Albatross* is the second in line) was the terror of the skies over the Western Front in 1916-17. Like many other flyers, Richthofen began the war as a cavalry-man. In the Sixties, the "Red Knight" made a surprising reappearance in *Peanuts* comic strip.

At right: An artist's later impression of the last combat of the flying idol of Germany. Richthofen, sandwiched between the two Canadians, never knew what hit him. "Wop" May (in the first plane) survived to become Canada's best-known bush pilot. He flew the first scheduled air mail into the Arctic.

Roy Brown – one bullet won him a niche in the hall of fame. But he collected eleven other scalps besides Richthofen's.

Manfred von Richthofen – he was summoned by his Kaiser for congratulations in 1917. **Below:** he meets the Empress, too.

The drama of Roy Brown and the Red Knigh

It is one of the great tales of Canadian arms. The invincible, arrogant Baron von Richthofen, patrolling with his *Jagdstaffel* 11 above the Somme Valley on an April Sunday in 1918, spotted a lone Allied plane far below. He had by now perfected his pitiless killing technique. With his squadron flying cover, he put his scarlet-nosed Fokker triplane into a steep dive, in anticipation of his 81st victim. His quarry was an inexperienced Canadian lieutenant named Wilfred May (but nicknamed "Wop"). As the planes roared over the trenches only 150 feet up, eyewitnesses could see the German tracer finding May's

plane. May was helpless, without even a hope of fighting back. His gun was jammed. But, this day, May had a pal with him. Capt. Roy Brown, from Carleton Place, Ont., had been just offstage keeping an eye on the newcomer. Brown flashed his Sopwith *Camel* on to Richthofen's tail and opened up. One bullet found the German's heart. The Red Knight was dead, at 26.

Roy Brown was given the seat from Richthofen's plane as a trophy. Today, it is displayed at the Royal Military Institute, Toronto. You can put your finger through the bullet hole.

CURRIE

Official portraits flatter. Lieutenant-General Sir Arthur Currie, commander of the Canadian Corps, never presented a very soldierly figure. Over 200 lbs, his girth defeated the tailors; from the rear, he resembled one of the first lumbering tanks. His heavily jowled face seldom knew a smile. He was, nonetheless, an authentic military genius: an Ontario farm boy, a schoolteacher, an incautious real-estate speculator who proved spring steel in the acid test of war, leading men with a flinty resolution and sharp intelligence in a conflict that destroyed the most renowned reputations of the age.

On the flyleaf of his diary, Currie had written: "Thorough preparation must lead to success. Neglect nothing." British Prime Minister Lloyd George had favoured Currie's appointment if it had been decided to replace Sir Douglas Haig as Commander-in-Chief.

Currie had friends in high places, but he also had an implacable enemy: Sam Hughes, the erstwhile Minister of Militia in Ottawa. Currie had come out against the Canadian-made Ross rifle, a pet project of the Minister's, and he had also flatly refused to accept Hughes's son Garnet, as a front-line commander. The younger Hughes raged: "God help the man who goes against my father!"

HUGHES

"There is only one feeling as to Sam, that he is crazy." This is how Sir George Foster summed up the man who, above all others, ordered the Canadian war effort for nearly three years. Hughes' megalomania seems distressingly apparent today – and was obvious to many at the time – yet Hughes, a small-town publisher, created himself "War Lord of Canada." In South Africa. he demanded a Victoria Cross for himself; now, he swiftly collected a knighthood and the rank of lieutenant-general.

At the outset, Hughes threw away the mobilization plans, called regular officers "bar-room loafers." He seriously discussed taking personal leadership of the Corps at the front. He was finally sacked late in 1916.

The best thing Sam Hughes did was, in the three years before 1914, to raise Canada's military expenditure from $7 millions a year to $11 millions – thus improving training facilities. The worst thing was his vicious campaign to smear General Currie as a man who sought self-glorification in ordering unnecessary attacks, thus "needlessly sacrificing" the lives of Canadian soldiers.

The Minister of Defence enjoyed handing out promotions on the spot.

King George V walks in the mud of Vimy Ridge while the Canadian commander sticks to the boardwalk. Gen. Sir Henry Horne, First Army, is at right.

Sir Sam Hughes strides ashore in France to review his troops. His Special Representative at the Front was Sir Max Aitken, the future Lord Beaverbrook.

Dumbells Concert Party, organized from serving soldiers, grew sophisticated when costumes were contributed. They began with *Oh, What a Lovely War* and at the Armistice were producing Gilbert and Sullivan operettas.

Men of the Fourth Division make instant friends with the ladies of Saudemont, a village they liberated – after four years of German occupation – between Arras and Cambrai. The Allies were now rolling towards victory.

The *Maple Leaf,* published in England for Canadian servicemen in the C.E.F., Navy and Flying Corps, was a link with home. Several of its writers and editors became big names in the nation's newspapers after the war.

Taking time out from the war – the rumble of the guns was always a faint distant thunder – these Canadians help out on a French farm. Attractions included fresh air, fresh vegetables and . . . a certain *je ne sais quoi.*

A French boy peddles out-of-date English newspapers to the Canadians. This photo has all the earmarks of the press relations officer: the purchaser is Pte. Tom Longboat, Canada's famed Indian long-distance runner.

Behind the lines: Canadians relax with mademoiselles from Armentieres, or Anyplace

Horsing it up, Drivers W. Scott and S. C. Worley amuse the crowd at the Canadian Corps horse show on July 19, 1916. Seven thousand horses had sailed from Quebec with the first contingent but the day of the war horse was already over.

Poker, blackjack, spit-in-the-ocean, seven-toed Pete, these were the games the troops got up as soon as they moved into the rear after they had finished their trick in the line. Some of the games – they called them "schools" – floated from one sector to another, astronomical losses being carefully calculated and then the slate silently wiped clean when the next patrol reduced the circle of players.

They could get simple fun out of anything, including the place names along the front. Even French Canadian officers preferred *Wipers* to Ypres and *Plug Street* to Ploegsteert. Arras fared poorly in this game. Canadian gunners chalked "Iron Rations" on shells scheduled for the enemy. Their humour was suitably sardonic. They roared the song about the ancient charms of the *mademoiselle* from Armentières (*"par-lay voo?"*) and delighted in the Dumbells' version of, "I've got a motter/always merry and bright." "Pack up Your Troubles in Your Old Kit Bag" was as good advice as any, under the circumstances. Helping keep up civilian (feminine) morale was a Canadian specialty.

The Dumbells Concert Party, organised by Merton Plunkett of the Y.M.C.A. in 1916 from serving soldiers of the Third Division, became the standard by which all the divisional entertainment groups were judged. The first Dumbell concert was given at Poperinghe, Belgium, with nearby artillery providing "noises off." For an all-male audience, it included a transvestite turn and, after that, female impersonators were always featured.

With the Volatiles (the First Division entertainers), the Dumbells put on a great show on Dominion Day, 1918, just before the Canadians pushed forward in the last great attack of the war. Under an umbrella of Royal Air Force planes, 50,000 men had gathered at Tincques, near Arras, to watch sports, Highland games, massed bands, and to be inspected by Prime Minister Borden and General John J. ("Black Jack") Pershing, Commander-in-Chief of the newly-arrived Americans. The Dumbells survived demobilisation and became the first Canadian revue to storm the fortress of Broadway.

The gaunt ruins of the ancient city of Cambrai – once Germany's defence pivot – are still burning as a Canadian platoon crosses the central square.

Huge howitzer shells (up to 15 inches diameter) lobbed into Arras, familiar to Canadians as the stepping-off place for Vimy Ridge. The capital of the Artois kings and birthplace of Robespierre took a final belting in the German offensive of 1918.

Ruined towns, a charred countryside —
the legacy of war

For three years, the front lines never moved more than five miles and there the earth was scorched into a wasteland in which a splintered charred tree, still standing defiantly, was an object of remark. It was mostly a country of small farms, orchards, woods and villages, many of which simply disappeared forever. The few sizeable towns within artillery range – Ypres, Lens, Loos, Albert, Cambrai, Arras, Amiens, Soissons – were partly or wholly reduced to rubble.

The most-publicised destroyer of the war was Big Bertha, a gun with a range of 75 miles, named for Bertha Krupp, daughter of the manufacturer. In fact, although she threw 400 shells at Paris, Bertha did surprisingly little damage. Canadian artillery did more than its share. Brigadier-General A. G. L. McNaughton (who would lead a whole Canadian army two decades later) wrote, in the inescapable jargon of the Services: "I know of no organization in the history of war which was able to produce such a high ratio in shell to troops." Translation: Canadians fired more per man.

Another shell adds to the devastation on the Somme. These are the ruins of Courcelette, taken at the point of the bayonet in 1916 by French Canadians and Nova Scotians. "If hell is as bad as Courcelette," an officer wrote, "I would not wish my worst enemy to go there."

The Hundred Days: last act of the long trial

The end began with the discovery of a tactic the Iroquois or the guerrillas of the *Ancien Regime* could have taught the High Command: surprise. At dawn on August 8, 1918, the Canadian Corps, without signalling its punch in any way, leapt forward from Amiens, brushing the German defences aside. They drove eight miles, capturing 5,000 prisoners. Australians and French on the flanks had similar successes. Planes had flown back and forth at night to cover the noise of tanks clanking into position.

The German nation was visibly crumbling from the long-term effects of the blockade at sea and the appalling casualties of the Western Front, but, even so, the field-grey soldiers of the Kaiser turned and fought desperately

Snipers bullets keep this Canadian's head down at the vital rail junction of Cambrai. A brilliant crossing of the Canal du Nord outflanked the city.

A Canadian patrol enters Valenciennes, where the enemy made a determined stand. General McNaughton's heavy artillery pumped 2,149 tons of shells into the German positions at outlying Mont Huoy and, as the 10th Brigade swept through, Sgt. Hugh Cairns of the 46th Battalion won the last Victoria Cross of the war.

at many points during the next three months as they were harried and routed by the victory-flushed Allies. The Americans drove through the Argonne with great dash and the Canadians pierced the feared Hindenburg Line in seven days. Here, Major Georges Vanier, later to become Governor-General of Canada, lost his right leg.

Admittedly only one corps amid whole armies, the Canadians kept up the running through Douai, Cambrai, Denain, Valenciennes and Mons. It all ended there, in the cobbled Grande Place of that Belgian town, with General Currie taking the salute on horseback. His troops blushed to the colour of the red carnations that girls had stuck in their caps when the joyous citizenry shouted, *Vive les braves Canadiens!*

The pipers of the 42nd Battalion play through the streets of Mons on the morning of November 11, 1918. The flags had been kept hidden by the Belgians for four years. Already, troops of the Second and Third Divisions had pushed beyond the town. All firing ceased at exactly 11 a.m.

The first item on the balance sheet for the 1914-18 War is in red – 60,661 Canadians lost their lives, nearly ten percent of the total enlistment. When misty-eyed children stood up in schoolrooms across the nation and recited the most famous poem of the war, written by a Guelph, Ont., doctor, Colonel John McCrae . . . *We are the dead. Short days ago / We lived, felt dawn, saw sunset glow, / Loved and were loved, and now we lie / In Flanders fields* they were often speaking of a father or a brother. McCrae, who had fought in South Africa, himself died in a Canadian hospital in France in January 1918.

The total enlistment in all services reached 628,462. This meant that 13.48 percent of the male population was in uniform, not all of them willingly. The introduction of conscription in 1917 must be counted a regrettable failure as it served to deepen Anglo-French differences without adding appreciably to the flow of dependable troops. (It should be added that this is not the official view.) Prime Minister Borden was pushed into conscription by statistics like these: At Vimy Ridge, in April 1917, the Canadians suffered 10,602 casualties in six days; in that whole month at home, the total of recruits numbered 4,761 – even with red-blooded Canadian girls handing out white feathers in the streets. In the fighting at Lens, 5,500 Canadians fell in four days. Compared with other Empire countries like Australia and New Zealand, Canada had sent proportionately fewer men into battle.

The Great War – as the struggle was designated until an even greater one began – cost humanity a total of 8,538,315 dead, 21,219,452 wounded and 7,750,919 missing or taken prisoner. Neither side bothered to count any civilians who got in the way. It was, in God's mercy, the only one of its kind.

After the first German thrust in the late summer of 1914 was turned back at the Marne, a scant 30 air miles from Paris, the straining masses of men sank into the mire of Flanders and Picardy and advances trumpeted in the censored home newspapers as great victories were, in grim reality, often only gains of a few pulverized Belgian or French farmyards. Soon, the opposing military commands seemed to be trapped – like two stubborn men in a revolving door. Nearly all the Allied advances of three years were more than wiped out in the suicidal German offensive in the spring of 1918. The attrition battles of the Somme and Passchendaele – in both of which Canadian manhood was recklessly spent – are particularly remembered with revulsion as typifying this most brutal and degrading of wars where the deliberate policy of reactionary high commanders was to try to outspend their opponents in flesh and blood.

Canadians were now regarded particularly as shock troops, best suited to attack and to exploitation of success where their supposed "frontier ingenuity" would break through inflexible army-school thinking. British Prime Minister Lloyd George later wrote in his *War Memoirs:* "Whenever the Germans found the Canadian Corps coming into the line, they prepared for the worst . . ."

When the Allied victory was conceded – at the Armistice, not a single invader stood on German soil – the statesmen gathered at Versailles to tramp out the grapes of wrath. In doing so, to the last bitter juice, they ensured the resumption of the conflict. When that day came, just twenty years later, the new weapons that the Allied Command could not properly grasp on the Western Front were ready, and polished, in the German fist to start an entirely different kind of war.

Inset The 3rd Field Hospital at Doullens, France. In total, 21 Canadian hospitals maintained 13,500 beds in the war zones.

At right Strange shapes of a Canadian patrol – scene on the Aleutian island of Kiska in 1943.

3/THE WORLD WAR

3/ The World War

This time we took a headstart. On the sultry evening of August 25, 1939, ten thousand of Canada's civilian soldiers kissed their worried wives, picked up the rifles left over from 1918, and went on guard at airfields, canals, bridges and coastal defences across the country. The invasion of Poland, marking the resumption of open warfare at last by the revivified, revanchist German enemy was still six days away. However hollow the military's gesture – Canada possessed not even one modern anti-aircraft gun – it demonstrated with complete accuracy the grim but cool decision of the nation that it was time, and necessary, to go to war again. It seemed unbelievable that an unbalanced Austrian ex-corporal with a Charlie Chaplin moustache could have set Europe ablaze again but, after the seizure of Czechoslovakia in the spring, very few Canadians still believed that Adolf Hitler, and his Italian ally, Benito Mussolini, could be stopped by words alone.

The politicians, as sometimes occurs, were a distance behind public opinion. When British Prime Minister Neville Chamberlain returned from the infamous appeasement at Munich in the previous fall, Canada's Prime Minister, W. L. Mackenzie King, cabled him happily: "The heart of Canada is rejoicing tonight . . . The voice of reason has found a way out of the conflict." Socialist leader J. S. Woodsworth moved in Parliament that "in the event of war, Canada should remain strictly neutral, regardless of who the belligerents may be."

The German panzers, irresistible progeny of the tanks the British Command couldn't get the hang of in the first struggle, rolled into Poland on September 1, and, 48 hours later, Britain and France were at war again with the old foe. Mackenzie King had, reluctantly, shed his euphoria and was taking the country into the conflict but at a deliberate slow march designed to emphasize that Canada, eight years utterly independent of Britain, was taking its own decision. Parliament did not meet until September 7 and it was not until Sunday, the 10th, that the declaration of war was approved. Four M.Ps argued against it but

only Woodsworth insisted that his opposition be recorded.

This time, no-one sang *Rule Britannia*, or *La Marsellaise* either. No Sam Hughes strutted in sworded splendour. There were no torchlight parades, no huzzahs. That stuff had been okay for father, in the awkward adolescence of the nation; his son, older by a generation of disillusionment, shocked by the wasted sacrifice of 1914-18 and by the cynical circumlocutions of the League of Nations, simply stepped forward to get the job done. Properly, this time.

So many men volunteered that a large number of the recruiting depots had to be closed temporarily. At the outbreak, the strength of the Canadian professional armed services was: Army, 4,500; Air Force, 3,100; Navy, 1,800. At the end of September, the Army alone numbered 55,000, and the main problem was how to feed, clothe and equip them. War correspondent Ralph Allen reported the Army possessed 29 Bren guns, 23 anti-tank rifles and 5 three-inch mortars. Historian C. P. Stacey noted Canada possessed 14 tanks. The Navy had exactly 10 operational vessels.

When the war was over, six years later, 730,625 had served in the Canadian Army, 25,251 of them women; 249,624 men and women had worn the uniform of the Royal Canadian Air Force; 106,522 served the Navy (which, in 1945, had swelled to 400 ships). The enlistment was far greater than in the 1914-18 War but the cost was, mercifully, much smaller: 41,992 Canadians died – less than four per cent of the enlistment. General Isaac Brock, the victor of the War of 1812-14, who had once doubts about the Canadians' appetite for war, would have been humbled by this final statistic: 40.6 of the male population of Canada between the ages of 18 and 45 served in the armed forces.

When Winston Churchill announced the arrival by luxury liner of the 1st Canadian Division in Scotland just before Christmas 1939, the period known as "the phoney war" was current. Not a single bomb had been dropped on Britain, and the French officers, complacently secure within their Maginot Line, sipped fine wines and touched

72

snowy serviettes to their lips, then rose in elevators to inspect the guard.

When Hitler had digested his eastern conquests and when spring brought *Blitzkreig* weather, the war on the Western Front became realistic indeed. France fell in 43 days and only the minor miracle of a long calm in the Channel enabled the British to retrieve the 338,000 men who waded out from the Dunkirk shingle with only their rifles and revolvers. But for nearly all of the Canadians in Britain, eventually totalling a peak of 368,000, the phoney war lasted a soul-wearying, morale-eroding three years and six months; for more than half of them, it lasted even longer – four years and eight months elapsed from the declaration of war to the invasion of Normandy on June 6, 1944. It will always be the War of the Long Wait.

But not quite all of the Army sat and sulked. There were some now-forgotten, far-out forays. In April 1940, 1,300 troops of the 1st Division, including Princess Patricia's Canadian Light Infantry, first into action in the Great War, left by train for the Scottish port of Dunfermline to join a British force being rushed to threatened Norway. The Canadians had drawn the task of a frontal, seaborne attack on the port of Trondhjem, already in German hands. It was called off just before they sailed. *Lucky.* The soldiers saw it otherwise: they grumbled ferociously at the return to the bone-chill of Aldershot barracks where they had just endured the coldest winter Britain had known since 1894. The chance of a bullet with one's name on it was, to listen to most of the Canadians, preferable to zero weather in England's uninsulated housing.

Six weeks later, Major-General Andrew McNaughton's Division was moving again. This time, to France! The whole scheme, at this distance, seems quite mad. The British Army had already been pushed out of Europe at Dunkirk and the Germans were entering an undefended Paris. The plan was to try to keep a big toe-hold in France by forming a fortress area in the broad peninsula of Brittany. One Canadian and one British division, plus

The invasion of Sicily and Italy in 1943 finally broke the Long Wait of the impatient Canadian forces.

some escapees from Dunkirk, were to try to hold a line 150 miles long, through the provincial capital of Rennes. With the military and civil machine of France collapsing about them, the leading Canadian brigade pushed ever further inland, from Brest to LeMans. Then, in an atmosphere that must have reminded them of the 24-hour racing classic itself, they about-turned and drove pell-mell back to the channel coast. General McNaughton, who was still in Plymouth, was very busy seeing the Toronto Scottish aboard for France when word finally got to *him* that the show was cancelled. Only one brigade had actually embarked and they all got back except six, but the partial loss of weapons and transport (216 Canadian vehicles were ditched) was serious to an England patrolled by Home Guards with BB guns.

The interminable mock battles – they called them *Tiger, Fox, Spartan, Harlequin* – of the Long Wait chased the bored Canadians up and down the crowded, hungry island while they read enviously of the faraway excitements of Greece, North Africa and Russia. They had watched the Battle of Britain being fought, and won, above their heads. The frontrunners of the R.C.A.F's eventual 48 fighter squadrons got into the last rounds of that glorious scrap, notching 31 victims for the cost of 16 Hurricanes.

The Army's mounting sense of frustration caused many a punch-up in English pubs as 1941 passed in a bloodless tedium. Even a promising summer sally to Spitsbergen by a 2nd Brigade party of 500, with 100 Brits and Norwegians, turned into a fizzle when it transpired the enemy didn't even know the raid had taken place.

When contact with the enemy was finally made it was on the other side of the world. In September 1941, the British asked Canada to contribute two battalions to bolster the garrison at Hong Kong and General H. D. G. Crerar, then Chief of the General Staff at Ottawa, selected the Winnipeg Grenadiers and the Royal Rifles of Canada. They sailed from Vancouver on October 27, nearly 2,000 strong, and went into barracks at Kowloon. The Japanese struck Pearl Harbour and Hong Kong just

after first light on December 7. The Americans at Pearl Harbour, tragically, were taken completely by surprise; the Canadians and British at Hong Kong, just as tragically as it turned out, were standing waiting at their guns.

It was all over on Christmas Day. Completely isolated, short of water and ammunition, defenceless to air attack, the garrison surrendered. The Canadian toll was 290 dead, and in the harrowing years of imprisonment that followed another 264 men perished. Canada had seen blood at last – too much of it, in a dubious cause. Violent criticism at home caused the Government to appoint a royal commission to investigate: Was it ever likely two more battalions would deter the Japanese Army? The report was a whitewash for the authorities but, nonetheless, the affair is now clearly seen as a fool's errand.

The following year, 1942, is described by a single word in the Canadian military memory: Dieppe. Twenty-five years later, the raid by the 2nd Division on the French resort town at 4:50 a.m. on August 19, 1942, was still the most debated act of the whole war. It has been called "a majestic fiasco," "sheer bloody murder," and, by Winston Churchill, as "an indispensable preliminary to full-scale operations." General Crerar later rated the attack "a Canadian contribution of the greatest significance to final victory." A general named Montgomery, originally slated to lead the raid, advised calling it off. It is a debate for experts, and it is the experts who disagree so violently. The present writer adds only that Dieppe offers yet another example of the urge to arms, the calm acceptance of short odds, that has characterised the Canadian civilian soldier throughout his story. The deeds of that forlorn day can stand with Balaclava and with Actium. Nearly five thousand Canadians went to Dieppe; 2,211 got back to England, many of them wounded.

The thirst for action soon returned in the passing of yet another year of guarding England's shore against the invader who would never come and, when General Bernard Montgomery – now the glamorous victor of North Africa – led his Eighth Army against Sicily, the Canadian

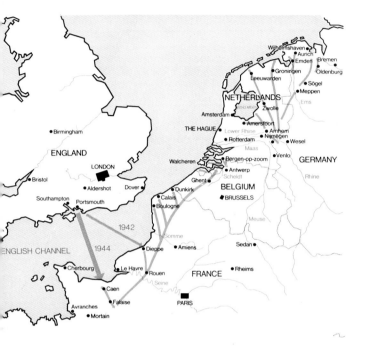

The Canadians made three cross-Channel forays into Europe: in 1940, a quixotic attempt to hold Brittany; in 1942, to Dieppe; in 1944 (broad arrow), to the D-Day beaches.

Government virtually insisted that he include our 1st Division and 1st Tank Brigade. Further, when the British and American forces pushed on into the toe of the Italian boot, on September 3, 1943, Ottawa also sent him the 5th Armoured tanks and the 1st Corps Headquarters. Monty accepted them less than politely (he really needed infantry). The position so stubbornly fought for by the Canadian generals in the 1914-18 War – that the Canadians must fight as a unified national force – was thus cheerfully abandoned. The G.O.C., General McNaughton, disapproved so strongly that he resigned.

At any rate, the Long Wait was over. For the next 20 months until, like the cornered scorpion, Hitler killed himself in his Berlin bunker, Canada could read with pride of the daily exploits of its forces in the field. The key campaigns from Sicily to the Scheldt, from Agira to Arnhem, the crescendo of D-Day when the 3rd Division hit the beach in Normandy, the relentless mainly-Canadian war on the U-boat in the western Atlantic, the numbing aerial attack on the German war machine— these great and stirring events are recorded in detail in the picture stories that follow. As at Mons in War I, the Canadians were face-to-the-enemy at Aurich at the final minute of War II in Europe, as the two Canadian corps commanders, Lieut.-General Guy Simonds and Lieut.-General Charles Foulkes accepted the surrender of the German forces on their north-western fronts.

Again, while other and older states declined, Canada had advanced in strength and stature in the show of arms in right cause. The close alliance with the United States, for the last three years of the struggle, cemented the security of the homeland and encouraged still further the natural unanimity of the peoples of the continent – not, in the view of a vocal minority, a total blessing. The rest of the world, soon to be dismayed by the fall of the Iron Curtain between East and West, between Communism and Democracy, began to look often to Canada for new ideas and, with touching faith, for a certain measure of idealism.

Overleaf: Bedford Basin was where the shooting war really commenced. The convoys assembled here, then passed out of the haven of Halifax harbour to brave the U-boats as they carried more troops and tanks to beleaguered Britain.

The first Tribal class destroyer built in Canada gets a lusty launching from the wife of the Navy Minister at Halifax. They carried the armament of prewar small cruisers and earned an honourable place in naval annals. One of the most successful, H.M.C.S. *Haida,* became a tourist attraction moored at Toronto docks.

Beneath the grey seas, a vicious killer

The day Britain declared war, a German submarine sank the Atlantic liner *Athenia* without warning, and the U-boat war was on. This time, Canada–with no seafaring tradi-

The war came to North America, sharp and shocking, when 200 ships were torpedoed within sight of land. In the map **above** the circles indicate sinkings and the few crosses, U-boat deaths. Commander Paul Hartwig took his U-517 into the St. Lawrence, 200 miles from Quebec City, and sank 30,000 tons on one trip.

Depth charges explode behind a Canadian ship on the Atlantic. The explosives had to hit within 20 feet of a submerged U-boat to hurt it seriously. Ten were laid in a diamond pattern with some timed to explode above the quarry, some below. The Germans would release oil, even wreckage, to suggest a casualty.

tion of its own–brashly accepted the job of safeguarding the first 1,000 miles of the Atlantic. In the first year, the U-boats sank 1,000 ships and the Germans were building eight subs for every one they lost. The establishment of the convoy system, improvements in radar and asdic underwater detection, and co-operation with long-range patrol aircraft dropped the rate of Allied loss by 1943 to 1 ship in every 344 convoyed. In two months that year the Germans lost 60 U-boats and, from then on, were in retreat. In total, Canadians made 27 kills.

The victim, U-210, just before she was rammed by the Canadian destroyer *Assiniboine (foreground)* on August 6, 1942, 500 miles from Newfoundland. For 35 minutes the two craft blasted pointblank. "We threw everything at him but the potato masher," a crewman said. Then *Assiniboine* rammed, twice.

How the corvette came, and conquered

"I do not like 'whaler', " rumbled Prime Minister Winston Churchill. "They are not going to catch whales." So they dusted off the name of an 18th-century French man o'war and called the new craft the corvette. Nevertheless, they *were* whalers, from the simple design of William Reed, and Canada built more than one hundred of them and threw them into the huge Atlantic seas to seek out the sleek, whale-like U-boats beneath the surface.

Bucketing out of St. John's and Halifax at the peak of the Battle of the Atlantic, the 190 ft. 16-knot corvettes played a major role in the victory. But they were hell to live in as they raced through mountainous grey seas –often cloaked in twelve inches of ice–on the track of a suspected submarine. Their bite was the 300lb depth charges they dropped in patterns, trying to crack the double skin of the enemy below. The corvette sailor–often a prairie boy–didn't spend his shore leave improving his swimming: he knew that on the North Atlantic convoy route he would last just five minutes in the icy water, even if he could swim like a champion. Canada's Navy eventually had 400 ships in commission and they shepherded 25,343 merchant ships across to Britain.

Pom-pom guns on H.M.C.S. *Drumheller* alert for dive-bomber attack. Naval fatalities totalled 1,797 and 95 became prisoners of war.

Opposite Below decks, the small ships seemed smaller yet. It was no place for the introvert, yet boys quickly became men and an *esprit de corps* developed. Jack Nicholls painted this lively scene.

Just about every Canadian wartime sailor knew this view of St. John's. The port could find 100 girls for an instant dance.

The years of the Long Wait

The first Canadian troops arrived in Britain before the end of 1939, expecting, like their fathers before them, to proceed to France to fight the German invader. The great majority of the expeditionary force, however, did not reach France until more than four years later. In the long meanwhile, they had to struggle with a different enemy: *ennui*. During the first period of the Long Wait, when the Canadians made up the only fully-armed mobile force available, there was excitement and threat enough. The question was not *if* Hitler would unleash his *Sea Lion* plan for the conquest of England, but only *when*. While the rest of the world watched breathlessly, the Battle of Britain was won in the air and the Royal Navy kept command of the Channel. *Der Fuhrer* called off the invasion on September 17, 1940. The long subsequent haul of training and retraining, of leaves in battered, rationed Britain, the natural frustration of a fighting army stuck in Sussex while other Commonwealth soldiers were at grips with the enemy—these elements bore heavily on morale. Hitting out when they could, army gunners downed eight German planes over England.

This Canadian band in Trafalgar Square must have played *There'll Always Be an England.* **Opposite:** Obeying the order of the day—wait.

The mistake at Hong Kong

"If Japan goes to war there is not the slightest chance of holding Hong Kong or of relieving it. It is most unwise to increase the loss we shall suffer there . . ." This was written (by Winston Churchill) nearly a year before the Japanese attacked Hawaii. Nevertheless, nine months later, two Canadian battalions arrived at Hong Kong to stiffen the garrison and, with grim exactitude, they did "increase the loss." The move was intended, incredibly, to deter Japan, already an obvious subscriber to the Berlin-Rome-Tokyo Axis, from entering the war. When the attack did come, the main line of defence–it was called the Gin Drinkers' Line–soon crumbled. The scratch defence force of 10,000 did inflict 2,754 casualties on the invaders but the result was never in doubt. Nearly half of the Canadian loss of 554 men was incurred in the prison and work camps where conditions were appalling. Four soldiers were shot for trying to escape; a diphtheria epidemic killed another 50 who were denied proper medical care. Several Japanese commanders were, after the war, given life sentences for barbarism.

Pictorial record of ill-treatment meted out by Japanese was made by a Russian. **Opposite:** Watching sunset, the event of the day.

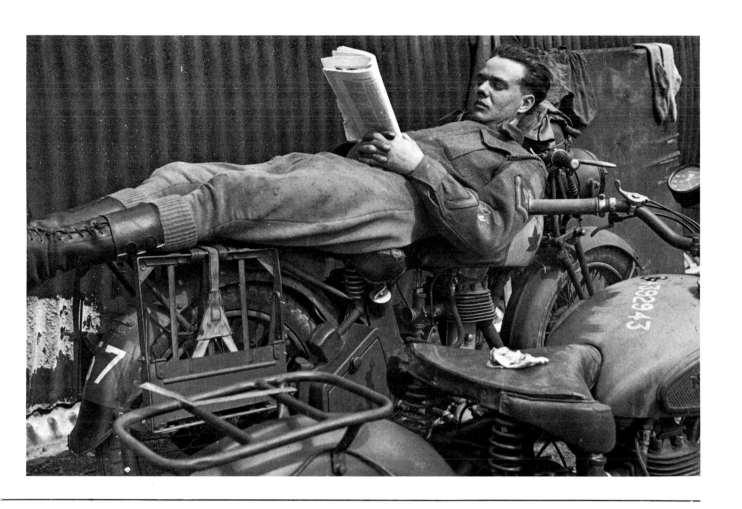

A.V. SKVORZOV JUNE 1945.

Royal Hamilton Light Infantry rush toward the Dieppe Casino. Artist Charles Comfort included tanks but, in fact, they arrived 15 minutes late.

The bitter victory of Dieppe

At least eight books have now been written about the Canadian raid on Dieppe in the mid-summer of 1942 and a $5 million motion picture on the subject has been announced. The episode will probably always remain a focus of controversy because the question it poses cannot be answered with certainty. Did the raid, which failed in its stated purpose (to seize the port and hold it until dark), actually provide the Supreme Command with vital experience for the Normandy invasion? A great number of great men say *yes, it did!* They include Admiral Earl

Mountbatten of Burma who, as Chief of Combined Operations, planned the attack. "If I had the same decision to make again, I would do as I did before," he says today. "It gave the Allies the priceless secret of victory."

Could such a continental port, then considered immediately essential for the success of any invasion, be seized by surprise frontal blow? Heartily sick of the Long Wait, the Canadians were eager to try. The six infantry battalions of the Second Division, under Major-General J. H. Roberts, a tough-minded British Columbian, were chosen to get an answer to the question. They were accompanied by the 14th (Calgary) Tanks, 1,075 British commandos and some 50 American Rangers (as observers).

They rushed in from the sea at the few breaks in the

It was all over at 1.30. Germans took these photos of their success.

Captors credited Canadians with Angriffsfreudigkeit (fighting spirit).

shore cliffs, without preliminary bombing or bombardment. The 302nd German Infantry Division, utterly taken by surprise but superbly positioned to sweep the beaches, proved to them in nine awful hours that such a port could not be seized in such a manner.

The "priceless secret" of Lord Mountbatten's was, then, that invading troops would in future need heavy fire support from sea and air; that a more specialized naval force was required for beach assaults; that the artificial harbours under study should be proceeded with. The price of this was, for Canada, 907 lives. The large number of 1,944 men surrendered and spent the next three years in German prison cages. They included a colonel and a chaplain who had each earned the Victoria Cross.

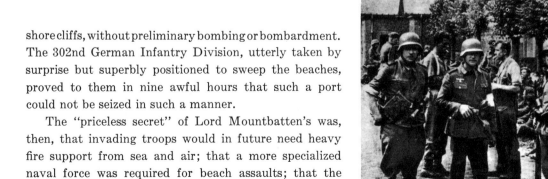

Prisoners were shackled in a bitter dispute and Canada took reprisals.

Are you the Girl he left behind?

Are you the girl he said he'd come back to, just sitting, dreaming of the day when he'll come back home again? Then, here's the chance to show him that you are made of the same kind of stuff—that you, too, have a sense of obligation and duty. Women are urgently needed in the Canadian Women's Army Corps to release men for combat duty. There's a job there waiting for you in the C.W.A.C., a job he'll be proud to know you are filling and it's a job you'll like.

In addition to your regular army pay, with uniforms, you receive free dental and medical care and a special sum each month for personal requisites.

Allowances are also paid for dependent parents, brothers or sisters, and wives of service men may now retain their separation allowance when they themselves join up.

For further information apply to your nearest Recruiting Office.
This does not obligate you to enlist.

join the
CWAC

Canadian Women's Army Corps

The gentler sex takes a hand

By the end of 1941, 1,200 women were gracing the uniform of the Canadian Women's Army Corps. Equality may have been on the march–officers in the three women's services were supposed to rate salutes–but not in rates of pay. At the start, an enlisted "Quack" got 90 cents a day (an army private, $1.30). They drove trucks, did laundry, broke ciphers, handled mail. Eventually, 21,624 served in the C.W.A.C. alone, 2,891 of them going overseas to release men from headquarters jobs. First girls to enter a theatre of war were entertainers in the Canadian Army Show in Italy in May 1944. On the homefront, women welded 6,500 tanks and assembled 244,000 machine-guns.

A gentle hand was needed for this delicate weld.

At an arms factory: a sight to scare the foe.

The glamour of war. None of these trainees at Red Deer, Alta., ever felt quite the same after artist Molly Lamb painted them at gas-drill.

O Canada we stood on guard for thee okay

One of the strangest stretches of the World War was the period of two and a-quarter years when Canada was at war while the U.S., so close over the still-undefended border, was not. While Canadians in Windsor were being exhorted to save scrap metal and bones (see advertisements, **below**) Americans across the bridge in Detroit were throwing out old autos and enough old rags to clothe a British brigade. Advertising agencies writing copy for products sold in both Canada and the U.S. had to write queer things for the fighting Canadians. What, for instance, were these *coupons?* From 1942, Canadians had a ration-

You were coming home, dear

Your first leave! And I wondered, dear, if you'd still find me charming.

You used to love my hands. And—now—well everyone says that war work like mine takes the beautifying moisture from hand-skin.

I'd have hated, dear, to meet you with rough hands. I'm glad I didn't have to. One of the girls I work with told me about Jergens Lotion and I used Jergens faithfully, thinking of you. I saw my hands get softer and smoother.

I'm so happy—and grateful to Jergens. You still do love my hands.

Charming young wives of men in the Service use Jergens Lotion, nearly 3 to 1. Like professional hand care! Contains 2 ingredients many doctors use to help rough, chapped skin become nice and soft again. Easy; no sticky feeling. Always use Jergens Lotion.

ERGENS LOTION FOR SOFT, ADORABLE HANDS

It's not easy to manage everything **ALONE!**

WRITE TO HIM TODAY . .

Published by this magazine in the interests of

ing system by coupons for gasoline and sugar (½ lb. per person per week); liquor and nylons were hard to come by. We had wage and price controls and, between 1939 and 1944, income taxes increased more than ten times as we ran up a $15 billion bill for the war. Under the super-efficient American-born Minister of Supply, Clarence D. Howe, Canada made every one of the 2,000 items of equipment needed by the army; we could equip a division of infantry every six weeks. Howe started 28 crown corporations to break bottlenecks (and limit war profiteering). To the envy of the rest of the world, the Canadian cost-of-living rose only 19 percent (during the 1914-18 War, 54 percent). Nearly 800,000 motor vehicles were produced in Canadian factories and 1,100,000 persons were directly employed in war industry. For a nation then numbering just 11,507,000, it was a very tidy effort.

Interned because of his agitation against national mobilisation registration, the ebullient mayor of Montreal, Camillien Houde, was a supporter of Mussolini's. "If war should come between Britain and Italy," he had said, "French Canadian sympathies will be with Italy."

"Not necessarily conscription but conscription if necessary." Behind this flummery, Prime Minister Mackenzie King, convinced he was saving Canada from flying asunder, edged towards the inevitable draft for the army.

Through a plebiscite, the firing of a flock of ministers, minor rioting in Quebec, King finally ordered 12,908 home-defence troops (the volunteers called them "Zombies") to the overseas battlefield. In the last months of the war, about 2,500 of them were scattered into the 21 line battalions of the army where they did as well as anyone. The French-English strife that haunted the dreams of ageing politicians did not, of course, occur. Many "Zombies" chose that label proudly, because they *believed* that outright conscription was the only fair way to share the vital burden of war. The nation had matured since 1918 and was ready, in good cause, to act like a single nation.

The enemy who wasn't there

Ant-like columns straggle up the hills of Kiska from silent beaches.

On June 20, 1942, the Japanese submarine I-26 shelled Estevan Point, Vancouver Island. Nobody was hurt and practically no damage caused but the fear of major action against the country heightened. Earlier, the Japanese had set up bases in the Aleutian Islands, on the doorstep of North America. The 8th Division was organized for Pacific Coast defence and Major-General G. R. Pearkes, V.C., was brought back from Europe to take command. An armoured train, mounting two 77mm guns pointing seaward, made daily trips along the c.n.r. track between Terrace and Prince Rupert.

The Americans landed on Attu island in May 1943 and killed virtually every one of the 2,500 Japanese there. Now, 5,300 Canadians (mostly conscripted "Home Defence" troops) joined 30,000 Americans to take Kiska. The island was heavily bombed and bombarded, then the troops stormed ashore on August 15. Fiasco! There was no-one there. The Japanese had left two weeks earlier.

Canadians bns Yanks in the canteen line-up. Biting winds were the worst hazard on the 25-mile-long island. The U.S. Intelligence had a very red face.

Italy: At long last, at grips with the enemy

Canadians were not included in the plans for the invasion of Italy in 1943 but the nation decided the Long Wait had already lasted quite long enough. The 3rd British Division found itself displaced by the 1st Canadian Division for Operation *Husky*, the invasion of Sicily, the first phase. The men of the 1st Division, who had arrived in England three and a-half years earlier, were more than restless and looking for fight. Before Canada's part in the Italian campaign ended in early 1945, they got plenty of it.

With the Shermans of the 1st Armoured Brigade, the Canadian infantry went ashore at Pachino, Sicily, on July 10, 1943, as part of General Montgomery's great Eighth Army. It was a good augury–the landing was virtually bloodless as the Italian rank-and-file had no stomach for Hitler's war (Mussolini was ousted on July 25). The men of the P.P.C.L.I., continuing their record of "first blood," captured the enemy commander at Modica after 48 hours' advance. German units on the island fought with expected stubbornness and the Canadians had several sharp battles, particularly on the hills at Agira.

When the Allies–the U.S. Fifth and the British Eighth Armies were both under the command of General Alexander, Governor-General-to-be–fought their way up the Italian mainland, the Canadian component was soon swelled by the arrival of the 5th Armoured Division.

"Whoever holds Rome," Churchill said, "holds the title deeds to Italy." Through Campobasso, Termoli, Pontecorvo, the Sangro, the Moro and Ortona, the Canadians played a fiery role along the many roads to Rome.

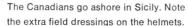
The Canadians go ashore in Sicily. Note the extra field dressings on the helmets.

Attacking up the Liri Valley towards
Rome – beyond embattled Cassino – the
Canadian Corps, commanded by
General Burns, reaches the Melfa River.
Here, Major J. K. Mahony of the Westminsters,
thrice wounded, won the V.C. King George,
travelling incognito as "General
Collingwood," gave him the medal in the field.

Christmas at Ortona

It was a Christmas dinner to be remembered always. In the midst of the battle the troops contrived a fair semblance of conviviality. The Seaforths laid their tables in the church of Santa Maria and the signals officer played carols on the organ. This photograph shows the brigade headquarters mess. The 48th Highlanders went hungry on Christmas Day, cut off during a flanking move outside the town. That night, a special party of the Saskatoon Light Infantry got through to them with their delayed dinner, not forgetting the candy, fruit and nuts.

Men of the 1st Division – these are
Edmontonians — enter the narrow streets of
Ortona. Nearly every house held an ambush.

The capture of the medieval stone town of Ortona, perched on a ledge over the Adriatic coast of Italy, at Christmas 1943, was the climax of three weeks of some of the hardest, and bloodiest, fighting ever experienced by Canadian soldiers. The two miles from the Moro River to Ortona cost more than 4,000 casualties and Major-General Christopher Vokes, now commanding the 1st Division, reported after the battle that every one of his nine battalions was at half-strength. They were some of Canada's most famous battalions–including the three professional army units, the P.P.C.L.I., the Royal Canadian Regiment and the Royal 22e Régiment. The 48th Highlanders were there, the Seaforths from B.C., the Loyal Edmonton, the Hastings and Prince Edward Regiment, West Nova Scotias, Saskatoon Light Infantry, and others just as renowned.

On the outskirts, near the Berardi crossroads, Captain Paul Triquet of the *Van Doos* won the highest decoration when he took on what seemed to be most of the 90th Panzer Grenadier Division with a party of 17 and four tanks.

When the fighting moved into Ortona on December 21, the Canadians were faced, for the first time in this war, with that exclusive infantryman's combat, the house-to-house battle. The steep streets, blocked with rubble, offered no way to tanks; artillery could seldom come to bear for fear of hitting the home team. Using explosives, or the portable Piat anti-tank gun, the platoon sections knocked holes through the walls of the adjoining houses and raced through the smoking gaps, machine-guns chattering.

On the 25th, the proximity of the enemy notwithstanding, the men of the fighting battalions insisted on their traditional Christmas dinner. One by one, the forward companies were relieved to stumble back for two hours each, to sit at white tablecloths and be served (by their officers) roast pork, apple sauce, plum pudding, candies and nuts. There was one bottle of beer per man— for some, resuming the combat with crumbs on their battledress, the very last beer in the world.

An anti-tank gun blasts down an alley at a German strongpoint. They fired pointblank into upper floors, knocking out machine-gun nests.

The streets were full of flame and fury. When the enemy pulled out on the night of December 27, he left 100 unburied dead.

The flying tradition: Canadians in the air war

"It drives one mad to think that some Canadian boor, who probably can't even find Europe on the globe, flies here from a country glutted with natural resources . . . to bombard a continent with a crowded population." So wrote the Nazi propaganda minister Josef Goebbels in 1943 when the Allied bombers, in ever-increasing numbers, began to pound the German war machine into flaming debris. The "boors" who continued to enrage him were the men of the 15 R.C.A.F. heavy bomber squadrons – and they could, incidentally, find any pinpoint in Europe on the darkest winter's night. They had behind them a Canadian flying tradition that went back to the *Silver Dart* in 1909 and they had learned their deadly craft with Canadian thoroughness on the prairies under the incredible Commonwealth Air Training Plan. This scheme, operated by the R.C.A.F. for five years, turned out 131,553 flyers and 106,000 groundcrew and was, without doubt, one of the greatest factors in the victory of the democratic powers. More than half of the graduates were Canadians, a third from Great Britain, while Australia and New Zealand were well represented. The C.A.T. Plan also trained free Poles, Czechs, Dutch, Belgians and Frenchmen.

Canadians flew every kind of plane there was – the workhorse *Dakotas*, the plywood *Mosquitos*, the glamorous *Spitfire*, the *Halifax*, *Liberator* and *Lancaster*, those lumbering engines of doom; apart from the bombing "milk runs" into the German industrial heartland, they flew with the Desert Air Force in the Middle East, on coastal patrol from Ceylon, over the Burma Road, the Norwegian fiords, and swept the Atlantic on U-boat patrol.

The air force that had started the war 3,100 strong, ended it with a roll call of 249,624. Seventeen thousand lost their lives; this number included six officers who were murdered in cold blood by the Nazi Gestapo when caught after the "great escape" from Stalag Luft III, in Silesia, on March 24, 1944. It also included Andrew Charles Mynarski, a leather worker from Winnipeg, who calmly spent his chance of living to try to get a friend out of a burning *Lancaster* in June of that same year.

Looking out through the nose cone of a *Halifax* Mark III bomber during a raid on the Ruhr. Artist Carl Schaefer made his colour sketches during an actual raid. "Model" is thought to be Donald Carr, of Fort William.

The airfield at San Giusto, near Pisa, Italy, gets a pasting from R.C.A.F. *Wellington* bombers – affectionately known as "Wimpies" – on September 22, 1943. The Canadians had dropped leaflets urging the Italians to quit.

The voices in the briefing room were low,
casual, with an off-hand ease so carefully
cultivated, but William Dring has caught the
tension in the faces of these Canadian
pilots about to take off on a mission.

Great deeds in the dangerous skies

"We have taken the very cream of the youth of Canada
... these boys are mainly third, fourth and fifth generation
Canadians ... they are the future leaders of this country
and the destiny of Canada will some day be in their hands."
This speaker, understandably prejudiced to air force blue,
was the Minister for Air, Charles Gavan Power, universal-
ly known as "Chubby." He was talking, in November 1941,
of the 90,000 young men already in the aerial war. They,
and the many thousands more who served in R.C.A.F. (and
R.A.F.) squadrons, went on to write a war record that
heavily underscored the now-mature might of the senior
Dominion. Billy Bishop, V.C., the great ace of the Great
War (now an Air Marshal), doffed his cap to them.

Acts of great courage in war are only seldom seen,
and even more rarely properly recorded, and this applied
particularly to the war in the air when a fighter pilot flew
alone and when a stricken bomber so often took all its
crew to a swift death. Occasionally, though, such acts
were caught for posterity to marvel at.

David Hornell, of Mimico, Ontario, was a mature 34
with 600 hours on his flying log when he put his clumsy
Canso flying-boat into the attack against a surfaced U-boat
off the Shetland Islands on June 24, 1944. The German's
guns again and again found Hornell's plane and his right
wing was in flames. He turned for another low pass and
dropped his depth charges right on the submarine. It
surged, broken, from the sea, then sank. The starboard
engine had now fallen off the Canadian plane but Hornell
calmly gained some height and then planed down for a
landing on the sea. The plane sank but one rubber dinghy
was saved, with not enough room for all the crew; they
took turns to tread water. After 21 hours in the icy sea,
they were rescued. Two crewmen were dead from exposure
and Flight-Lieut. Hornell died soon afterwards. He was
awarded the Victoria Cross, and all the survivors were
also decorated. That same month their squadron, No. 162
R.C.A.F., sank three more U-boats.

An aerial armada of 3,000 aircraft and gliders launched the attack across the Rhine, March 24, 1945. Nine hundred fighters covered the river crossings; the R.C.A.F. flew 200 missions.

At right Home-based squadrons covered the approaches to Halifax and the Gulf. Here, at Dartmouth, N.S., crashed *Hudsons* were stored in the "prang bins" as decoys in case of attack.

Lower left Inferno over Hamburg, pictured from a Canadian *Halifax* at 20,000 feet.

In the most agonizing decision of the war, Supreme Commander Dwight D. Eisenhower put the invasion back one day when the weather turned sour. Canadian tanks and cursing men had to spend 24 hours under camouflage nets on these landing craft.

The invasion of Normandy

One thing had been fixed since Dieppe: when the British and American armies stormed ashore along the Bay of the Seine on June 6, 1944, they were preceded by the most thunderous bombardment the navies and air forces

could deliver. Major-General R. F. L. Keller's 3rd Canadian Division hit the beach at Courseulles, Bernières and St. Aubin, in the centre of the British front. The Winnipegs, Reginas and Queen's Own bought the toughest patches on D-Day but it was a sparkling success all the way – and the total loss was one-third Dieppe's among three times as many men.

The bicycles were for the swift dash inland – Canadians hoped to make ten miles by nightfall. But Caen, only six miles inland, took a month to capture. Soldier at shoreline (*left of centre*) has just been wounded.

The spire of the church at Courseulles – a town that had known William the Conqueror – beckoned to the Canadians coming in over Mike Red and Nan Green beaches. At some places, the follow-up boatloads met more fire as the enemy recovered from shock. The bombing hadn't touched some defences.

"You will always remember with pride"

"All of us still fighting like mad . . ." This was part of the progress report sent back by the Canadian commander ashore in France to General H. D. G. Crerar, G.O.C., First Canadian Army. The British army commander, Lieut.-General Miles Dempsey, under whom the Canadians were fighting, had already written, "A battalion of 3rd Canadian Division was the first unit to reach the (D-Day) objective. That is something which you will always remember with pride."

Canada had much to remember. The first Canadians on French soil at the Second Front were "C" Company of the 1st Parachute Battalion, led by Colonel G. F. P. Bradbrooke. They jumped with the advance guard of the 6th Airborne Division, at twenty minutes after midnight. Badly scattered, the Canadians still destroyed all their allotted bridges and wreaked havoc behind the lines. Among the landing ships that brought the 3rd Division from England were the *Duke of Wellington*, *Queen Emma* and *Invicta*, all survivors of the Dieppe raid. They carried the smaller assault craft swinging at the davits; seven miles from shore the boats were lowered into a choppy sea, and, loaded with tense, determined (and scared) men, they headed for the beaches of Calvados. The assault craft had double bows, to help absorb explosions; some craft took 12 mines and still staggered on. Two Canadian destroyers, *Sioux* and *Algonquin*, were among the 105 warships hammering the coast defences held, on the Canadian front, by the luckless 716th German Infantry Division. When Le Régiment de la Chaudière at 8.30 a.m. rushed into the little resort of Bernières-sur-Mer, the townsfolk forgot their shattered houses in their delight at being liberated by men who spoke their own tongue. Finding the Courseulles beach exits jammed with men and vehicles, Lieut.-Colonel R. H. Webb lined up the guns of the 12th Field Regiment on the sands and blasted away right there. A lieutenant, a lance-jack and a private charged a pillbox that was chopping up the Q.O.R.; it was put out of action and they were gonged for gallantry.

All in all, it was quite a busy morning.

Canadian engineers run "mattressing" over the sand on D-Day beaches to assist vehicle landings. The tanks belong to the 1st Hussars (6th Armoured Regiment). Amphibious tanks, firing from the water, had given vital protection to infantry. No German planes appeared over the beachhead for nine hours.

As the invaders penetrated more deeply, German prisoners began to help with the evacuation of Canadian wounded. General Keller was later to be among the casualties. The British army had run into the most fanatical Nazi divisions – including Kurt Meyer's 12th S.S. – and the great Rommel was on the scene.

The end of the beginning

The role of the Canadians in Normandy–apart from the 3rd Division's on the beaches–was to provide the "follow-up army" that would break out of the bridgehead. But the Germans played a strong, iron hand and, within 48 hours, three armoured divisions had rushed forward to protect the pivotal town of Caen–and three more came later. While the Americans to the west made slow but steady progress, General Montgomery, as imperturbable and unhurried as ever, found his balance then threw everything he had into the capture of Caen: battleships at long range from the sea, 467 bombers, 656 guns wheel-to-wheel in the Alamein manner, three divisions of infantry. The town was taken on July 8/9, but only after

The civilians of Caen suffered grievously – about 350 were casualties and the greater part of the 9th-century town was destroyed. More by good luck, the church of St. Etienne, which William the Conqueror founded – and where he is buried – was spared.

One of the toughest tasks in the battle for Caen was the capture of the airfield at Carpiquet, on the outskirts of the town. The 8th Brigade – with an assist from the Royal Winnipeg Rifles — ran into a fanatical defence by the "Hitler Youth" of the 12th S.S. A seesaw battle for the ruined hangars (see **above**) went on for four days. In this action, the North Shore (New Brunswick) Regiment suffered its heaviest casualties of the whole European campaign. In proportion to the number of men engaged, the two Canadian divisions in the breakout battles paid the highest cost.

bitter fighting. Then, with the rest of their army now arrived from England, the Canadians joined the costly, often yard-by-yard, march down the arrow-straight road to Falaise. It was just beyond there, on August 22, after the enemy was caught in the American-British pincers and crushed in the Falaise Gap, that the Battle of Normandy was finally and completely won.

"Canadian Army will capture Falaise . . . It is vital it should be done quickly." This was para 10 of General Montgomery's order to his armies on August 11, 1944. It was begun through the wheatfields of the Laison Valley by massed tanks, mobile guns, with the soldiery going forward in armoured carriers.

A party of Les Fusiliers Mont-Royal with a tank of the Sherbrooke Regiment mops up in ruined Falaise, captured by Brigadier H. A. Young's 6th Brigade. About 60 "Hitler Youth" made a suicide stand in the high school buildings which were surrounded by a thick wall. Not one of them surrendered.

Major D. V. Currie, of the South Albertas (*left*, pistol in hand), during the desperate action at St. Lambert which won him Canada's first Victoria Cross of the campaign. With the heroic 1st Polish Armoured Division, the Canadians were preventing the enemy from fleeing the killing ground of Falaise.

The men of mercy

In this war of fast movement, fatalities were kept at a minimum by swift evacuation of wounded to casualty clearing stations, where emergency operations were performed. Then the patient moved by air or ambulance to any one of the 12 Canadian general hospitals established on the Continent. Another ten hospitals with more than 7,000 beds awaited serious cases in England. Nearly 3,400 Canadian nurses served overseas.

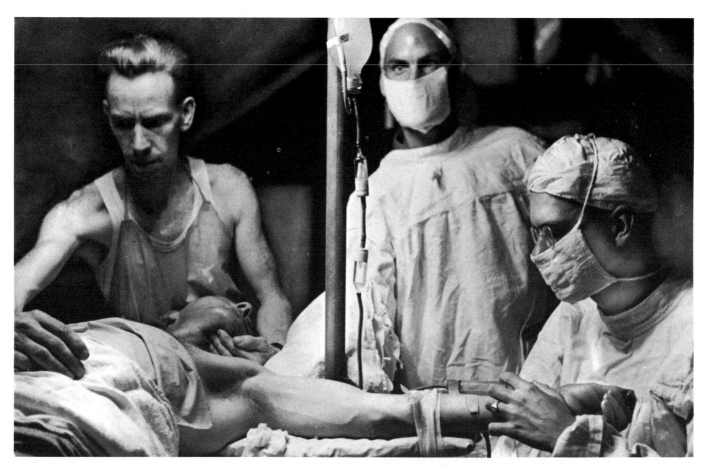

Surgeon Major F. G. Smith, R.C.A.M.C., (*centre*) in the operating theatre. Blood transfusions and German-invented sulphanilamides saved many lives.

Wounded in the attack on Keppeln, in the Rhineland, a Canadian is rushed out to a regimental aid post.

Religious consolation for a dying man.

The long left hook into Holland

The Canadian task was to clear the Channel ports – including an overjoyed Dieppe – and to open the entry to Antwerp. By Easter, the liberators were rolling into Holland (**below**).

An "alligator" with teeth of its own ferries men of the 3rd Division through flooded country near Nijmegen. **Bottom** Canadian artillerymen struggle in Dutch mud to realign their piece on a new target. A strange static period enveloped the front as the Allies prepared a final spring offensive.

The face of the vanquished: as Hitler's Reich crumbled, old men and mere boys were herded into the p.o.w. cages

Germany had started the war with two million men under arms, sure of their promised 1,000-year destiny. For two and a-half years — until the bloodbath of Stalingrad in the winter of 1942-43 — it seemed they had a chance of making it. The successive staggering losses on the Eastern Front and in North Africa — where Rommel's Army Group surrendered in

May 1943 – further diluted their strength before the Second Front was opened in Normandy in 1944. One-third of the 58 divisions awaiting the Allied stroke were purely defensive battalions including boys of 18 and younger, frost-bite cases from the Russian sector, men over 35 and even prisoners-of-war taken in the earlier eastern campaigns. The

Nazi officers, often still arrogant in defeat,
warned their Canadian captors
that someday all Aryans would have to
unite to fight the Communists.

real German punch was contained in ten
Panzer (armoured) divisions, several of them
highly-experienced, held in reserve for
counter-attacks. After the Battle of Normandy
was over, the enemy began scraping the
bottom of the manpower barrel. When the
Falaise pocket was sewn up by the First
Canadian Army, General Eisenhower reported:

"By 25 August the enemy had lost, in round
numbers, 400,000 killed, wounded or captured,
of which total 200,000 were prisoners of war
. . . 1,300 tanks, 20,000 vehicles, 500 assault
guns and 1,500 field guns and heavier artillery
pieces had been captured or destroyed." In
the noose thrown around the industrial Ruhr
by the Ninth and First U.S. Armies, 317,000

prisoners were taken, virtually wiping out the
two armies commanded by Field Marshal
Walter Model (who followed the example of
his predecessor Von Kluge by committing
suicide). In later battles the Canadians often
found, to their distaste, that they were fighting
boys who would have been in high school
back home. The total collapse was near.

The Canadians unite as the curtain comes down

With the arrival of the 1st Corps from Italy in April 1945, the Canadians fought the last few desultory battles as a united force. Often, the First Canadian Army–the name a proud national symbol–contained only a minority of Dominion troops. Men from the United Kingdom, Poland, the United States, Czechoslovakia, Holland and Belgium fought under our banner

A wounded Canadian is helped out of the line
in the last offensive. General Crerar had 400,000
men – the largest force ever commanded by
a Canadian. It included nine British divisions.
General Eisenhower said the action was
fought in "appalling conditions."

and, of the 67,787 casualties suffered by the army in the European campaign, more than one-third were non-Canadian. Germany remained a dangerous place until the last minute of the war – on the Canadian front, that was 8.00 a.m., May 5, 1945. Chaplain A. E. McCreery was one of 20 men killed on the 4th, and three were added to the honour roll on the 5th. The Queen's Own Rifles, in action at the last minute as they had been on the beach in Normandy, recorded with proper Canadian reserve: "There is no celebration but everybody is happy."

German prisoners assist elderly refugees back through the Canadian lines. The surrender was unconditional, the defeat – so different to that of 1918 – was complete. Field-Marshal Montgomery wrote generously of the Canadian effort, "They have proved themselves to be magnificent fighters, truly magnificent."

When the victory bells were still echoing over western Europe, 78,199 serving Canadians who hadn't had enough volunteered to fight the Japanese. Major-General B. M. Hoffmeister was appointed to lead the 6th Division into the Pacific, but the atom bombing of Hiroshima and Nagasaki brought the Japanese surrender before the Canadians got near the battle zone.

Peace brought men straggling back from all manner of places and from tasks that had been cloaked in secrecy. Some never did explain where they had been. Canadians with European and Oriental backgrounds served with several underground movements, as saboteurs and as Scarlet Pimpernels in arranging the escape of flyers shot down over enemy lands. French Canadian wireless operators, particularly, served with the Maquis, risking instant death – and sometimes torture – on discovery. Eight Canadian secret agents are known to have died in France; two parachuted right into the arms of the Nazi secret police following a betrayal in 1944.

One of the most remarkable units has been all but forgotten today. For two and a half years, 700 Canadians served within the U.S. Army's First Special Service Force. Raised originally to knock out power stations in Norway, the Commando unit served in the Aleutians, in Italy (the only Canadians in the vicious Anzio battle), and in the invasion of Southern France in August, 1944. If there had been any doubt of it, the special war of the 1st Canadian Special Service Battalion proved that Americans and Canadians merged almost indistinguishably. The guys with the accents were mostly Texans.

Young Canadian officers – 673 of them – responded eagerly in early 1944 when Britain was short of infantry leaders for the Normandy invasion. Known as the "Canloan," they wore the battledress of their new British units with an extra Canadian badge. In the thickest of the fighting, they behaved with great gallantry and suffered great loss (465 were casualties).

Another Canadian-British liaison that was to bear luxuriant fruit developed during the years of the Long Wait. Love affairs bloomed in black-out meetings, over a pint of warm ale in the Three Crowns or the Nag's Head, in the huge London dance palaces throbbing to the yearning songs of Vera Lynne. Canadian servicemen got married in bomb-bent registry offices, wooden chapels, wisteria'd village churches of Norman times and in St. Paul's Cathedral in the heart of London. By mid-1947, free transport to Canada had been provided for 40,764 war brides and their 19,608 children. Flying them "back home to see Mum" was to develop into a profitable trade for the air lines.

For a year after the war, Canada took part in the Occupation. From a headquarters near Oldenburg, where the final Canadian actions had been fought, more than 20,000 men of the Canadian Army Occupation Force performed the dispiriting drudgery of disarming and dispersing the utterly defeated German forces. Obeying the non-fraternization rules with the thousands of German girls starved for years of young male companionship was, at times, even more difficult. Canada had also sent overseas hundreds of Civil Affairs administration officers to work in liberated territory. These two activities, seldom mentioned in our national assessments, were to lead directly to Canada's main postwar military positions – the maintenance of a sizeable army and air force in Europe for a generation, and the seizure of a leading role in the new efforts of the new League of Nations to try to keep the peace by show of arms.

At right Under a new flag: The United Nations banner flies over the Imjin River, in Korea, 1952.

4/THE COLD WAR

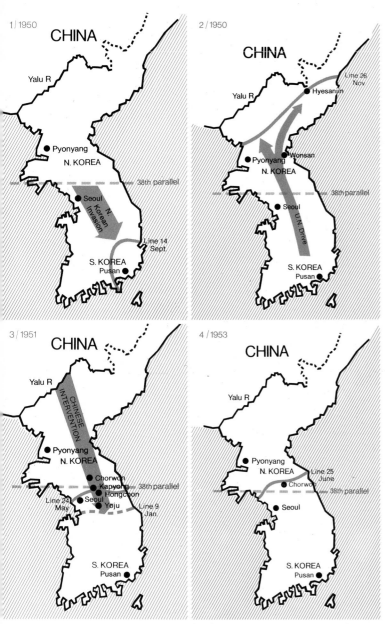

North Korea invades (map 1) on June 25, 1950;
the U.N. forces push them back 2); the
Chinese intervene directly (3); the line is
stabilized (4) near the old border.

The double-decker hangover from the celebrations of the absolute victories over Germany and Japan had barely subsided into a dull throb when Canadians – like democrats everywhere – began to realise they were already engaged in a different kind of war, a struggle that (since Hiroshima) could mean not merely victory or defeat for a nation or an alliance but for civilization itself. Winston Churchill had coined the chilling phrase "Iron Curtain" at Fulton, Missouri, on March 5, 1946.

The last Canadian troops returned from Europe late that year and, within months, Louis St. Laurent, then Minister of External Affairs, was warning that the Security Council of the still-shining-new United Nations, the only apparent hope of the world, was "frozen in futility and divided in dissension." When the Russians, openly grabbing a satellite empire as aggressively as any Caesar, Saladin or Hitler, did not like any measure before the Council they killed it with their veto.

Again it was the fate of Czechoslovakia, the orphan state in the cockpit of Europe, that shook most Canadians out of any remaining victory euphoria. The Russians had flatly refused to allow the Western nations to help the Czechs recover economically from the war and soon afterwards the Communists seized complete power, although they had received only a little more than one-third of the votes in the post-war election: The Czechs' idolized democratic president, Jan Masaryk, died in highly mysterious circumstances. St. Laurent was then the first to propose that, the U.N. Charter already torn, there should be "an association of democratic and peace-loving states willing to accept more specific international obligations in return for a greater measure of national security." St. Laurent was soon to become Prime Minister of Canada, but when that "association" was formed – it was to become known, simply, as N.A.T.O. – he was never credited as a founding father. Yet it was to be within the armed forces of the North Atlantic Treaty Organisation, facing the Communist front from the Baltic to the Black Sea, that Canada was to find, for the next generation, the continuance of its military record. Eventually, a French Canadian general, Gilles Turcot, would take over as commander of N.A.T.O.'s mobile strike force, the first unit to see action if the Communists ever risked further aggression.

The N.A.T.O. treaty, signed by 12 nations on April 4, 1949, marked the first time that sovereign Canada was committed in advance to go to war on foreign soil. Wartime Prime Minister Mackenzie King, an isolationist at heart, had refused to bind Canada to even the loosest general agreement for Commonwealth defence. Once again, war, this time the threats of the Cold War, had pushed Canada another steep step into the select and responsible company of major-league powers. However, before one Canadian soldier was sent back to Westphalia, a red-hot little war exploded in a place only a few could find on a map: Korea.

The Communist state of North Korea, created under Russian auspices out of half of the peninsula jutting off Asia into the Yellow Sea, its army hardened by Soviet one-party discipline, decided the time was ripe for a swift annexation of South Korea. The southerners were fooling about with democracy and, at a general election on May 30, 1950, they rejected all except a few of the Communist candidates. General Douglas MacArthur's supreme headquarters in Japan insisted the Reds would content themselves with border incidents. The U.N. already had a commission on the 38th parallel with a watching brief. So much for that. The North Koreans stormed across the border on June 25 and soon had over-run the whole peninsula, except for a salient at the port of Pusan.

One serious, and one fatal, miscalculation had been made by the Communists. The Americans were prepared to fight for that piece of rocky, barren real estate and, at that time, the Russians were boycotting the U.N. and therefore could not frustrate action by using their veto. President Harry Truman, an uncomplicated man with courage to grasp the nettle, ordered U.S. forces to help the South and the U. N. subsequently endorsed this action.

Canada immediately sent three destroyers from Esquimalt, soon afterwards an R.C.A.F. transport squadron, and, after what seemed to many to be over-long deliberation, announced on August 7 (43 days after the invasion) that an army brigade of 7,000 men would go to Korea as part of the U.N. forces. One reason for the delay: the two-corps Canadian Army of five years earlier had shrunk already to the equivalent of – well, one brigade. And, in the freezing atmosphere of the Cold War, this token force had some strange priorities: Minister of Defence Brooke Claxton had just ordered that units must wear dress uniform on ceremonial parades. That meant swords, Mac.

A special recruiting drive to raise troops for Korea was launched immediately and the Army demonstrated it had not lost its touch for foul-ups: the officer in charge of a Toronto recruiting depot arrived for work totally unaware of the Prime Minister's radio appeal the previous evening or of the black headlines in the morning press. What on earth, he wondered, were all these hundreds of men doing hammering on the door?

Trying to catch up the embarrassing time-lag, Brooke Claxton ordered that the depots speed the processing of recruits. This led to some hilarious results as adventurers and drifters grabbed the King's shilling. Col. H. F. Wood reports that one man of 72 and another with an artificial leg were enlisted. Nearly 1,400 men who had not been formally enlisted were found in Valcartier Camp. After wholesale discharges, about 8,000 men, nearly half of them veterans, remained, and Brigadier J. M. Rockingham, formerly of the 9th Infantry Brigade in World War II, back in civilian life as a business executive in British Columbia, accepted the command with 24 hours' notice. The politicians, with elaborate craftiness, had decided a civilian soldier like the popular "Rocky" would have greater appeal to recruits than a professional general, despite any rust that might have accumulated.

The Canadian Army Special Force, soon designated the 25th Canadian Infantry Brigade Group, moved into Fort Lewis, State of Washington, to train with the Americans under whose command they would fight. Lieut.-Col. J. R. ("Big Jim") Stone took the 2nd Battalion, Princess Patricia's Canadian Light Infantry, over to Korea just as the Chinese Communists intervened in the battle. In yet another war, the Princess Pats were determined to be the first Canadians to hit the enemy.

At the outset, the South Koreans were armed only with small arms and mortars; the Western Powers had refused them tanks, planes, even anti-aircraft guns. The Russian-trained North Korean Army, 130,000 strong, had 150 T-34 Russian tanks, plenty of light and heavy artillery and 180 Soviet Yak fighter aircraft. Even so, the scratch U.N. Army, now also including Britons, Australians, New Zealanders, Indians, Turks, and twenty other nationalities, was soon chasing the broken Northerners far above the border. A brilliant seaborne campaign at Inchon by American Marines, based on Wolfe's attack at Quebec, had turned the tide.

It was the world's first taste of a new warfare: turning words on their heads, it could only be called "fighting for peace." It was to become, as the Fifties merged with the Sixties, the main activity of the Canadian forces.

When the pursuit neared the Chinese-Korean border at the Yalu River, 180,000 Chinese infantry smashed into the U.N. forces without warning. The Canadians came into action for the first time south of Seoul, in the winter of 1951, when the Chinese assault was mostly stemmed. They winkled out guerrillas operating in the Naktong River Valley. Major C. V. Lilley wrote carefully in his report to Colonel Stone: "I consider hunting guerrillas the best company exercise . . . it brings out all the tactical and administrative lessons that have to be learnt."

Lilley had his company of Princess Pats on a key hill in the Kapyong Valley when the Chinese mounted their last major assault. Spurred on by their curious bugle calls, the Chinese attacked continuously during the night of April 24-25. Bren-gunner W. R. Mitchell, twice wounded, won the Distinguished Conduct Medal for his bravery that night, and morning found the Canadians still holding

firm. The battalion had suffered 33 casualties (ten of them fatal) and, on the forward slopes of the B Company position alone, there lay the bodies of 51 Chinese. President Truman awarded the battalion a Distinguished Unit Citation, the first time a Canadian unit had been so honoured. "Big Jim" Stone won a second bar to his Distinguished Service Order. The Kapyong Valley had been saved.

When the main body of the 25th Brigade reached Korea in May, 1951 – nearly a year after fighting had begun – the battlefront was already stabilising within a few miles of the 38th parallel, the original border. There would be some sharp actions as the U.N. forces slowly pushed the Chinese back to the Imjin River – the Royal Canadian Regiment and the *Van Doos*, Le Royal 22e Régiment, performed admirably in both defence and attack – but, mostly, the Korean War deteriorated into a wearing threat-and-bluster affair for the next two interminable years. Morale and fighting edge were almost impossible to maintain while stony-faced platoons of East and West negotiators were meeting off and on to arrange a cease-fire that would save sufficient face for the Chinese.

Canada's first experience of "fighting for peace" under the blue flag of the United Nations cost the lives of 294 men over a three-year period – one-fifth of Ontario's yearly highway death toll. The Dominion's representatives had won 234 honours and decorations, including eight D.C.Ms (regarded by some frontline soldiers as "just as good as" the Victoria Cross) and one George Medal. To national leaders yearning for Canada to cast a longer shadow on the world stage, it must have seemed an instructive experience.

On the European front, a Canadian brigade group and a division of fighter aircraft had arrived by Christmas 1951, to fulfil Canada's commitment in the N.A.T.O. force, then swollen to 14 participants by the recent addition of Greece and Turkey. Poor Czechoslovakia, twice the object of Canadian sympathy as it struggled against the oppressor, was now among the enemy, on the other side of Churchill's Iron Curtain, along with Poland, Hungary, Romania, Bulgaria and, of course, the mighty Union of

Soviet Socialist Republics (15 of them). The Eastern bloc powers formed themselves into a counter-N.A.T.O. association generally called the Warsaw Pact. With a steady show of muscle, sometimes flexed, oft-times quiescent, both West and East maintain the confrontation into the present.

A "Little Canada" has long since developed around Soest, southwest of Hanover, where the Dominion erected "forts" named *Henry, York, Beausejour, Chambly, St. Louis, Victoria,* and *MacLeod* to house the three battalions of the regular army that serve three-year stints on a rotation basis. The writer can verify that these troops, ignored by the homeland press for months at a time, execute their thankless tasks briskly and conscientiously.

Since the Communist bluff was called during the Berlin blockade and in the scares leading to the erection of the Berlin Wall, the East-West border has remained unchallenged. The internal unrest, and open rebellion, in Poland, East Germany and Hungary were so swiftly and ruthlessly put down by the Soviet forces that any Western supporting action beyond empty resolutions and heart-felt sympathy was still-born.

Action shifted to the Middle East. Present Prime Minister (then Minister of External Affairs) Lester Bowles Pearson won the Nobel Prize for his advocacy in 1956 of a United Nations military force which was inserted between the victorious Israelis and the defeated, Communist-armed Egyptians in the second of three attempts by the Arabs to destroy the Jews in biblical Palestine. Since Britain and France had, on this occasion, chosen to try to restore the Suez Canal to the status of an open-access international waterway (it had been built with that ideal), and to try to oust Egyptian dictator Gamal Nasser, Canada found itself in military opposition to the main forces of its own Queen. Five hundred Canadians, at first under General Burns, tried, with admirable patience, to help keep the desert peace for eleven years until the U.N. Secretary-General U Thant brusquely ordered them out, at the instruction of Nasser, clearing

the path for the Arabs' next disastrous, but nonetheless horrible, essay at genocide.

Canada had become, eagerly, the U.N.'s available policeman. In the brush-fire mini-wars that lit up the uneasy years of the Cold War, we had troops or airmen, or observers, or truce teams, in Vietnam (after the French defeat there), in Kashmir, in Cyprus, the Congo, in all the U.N.'s peace-keeping excursions (except New Guinea).

These years saw another development which, in the long run, is likely to prove selfishly closer to Canada's national interest. Ever since President Franklin D. Roosevelt exercised his famous smile on Prime Minister Mackenzie King at the 1940 conference at Ogdensburg, New York, setting the pattern for U.S. – Canadian co-operation in the World War, the two countries had moved into ever-closer defence collaboration. The Permanent Joint Board on Defence and the Military Co-operation Committee were established.

The U.S. Navy, Air Force and, latterly, inter-continental rocket system, have long since been quietly accepted by most Canadians as replacing the shield once provided by Her Britannic Majesty's Royal Navy. America, Roosevelt stated, would "not stand idly by" if Canada was threatened by anyone. If Hitler's armies had invaded and conquered England, the Canadian forces at home would have come under the control of the U.S. Army. After the war, joint military exercises were held in the Canadian North and the Americans paid the entire bill to throw the Distant Early Warning Line across Canada at the 70th parallel, a last-chance system to give the continent precious minutes to prepare for rocket war. In event of attack, our air force squadrons, and whatever secret anti-missile ordnance we may possess, will pass under the direction of North American Air Defence Headquarters at Colorado Springs.

In their centennial year, Canadians seemed happily content to cheer the Queen and her manly sea-faring Consort but to look to Uncle Sam to keep the wolves from their shores.

Undeclared but undoubted war in Korea

When the Cold War turned hot in the China seas, Canadians got their first experience of the new-style war: "fighting for peace." To the private in his foxhole, ducking the hardware flying about, it seemed suspiciously like any other kind of war. Before a patrol, still the same butterflies; afterwards, that indefinable elation. By the time the Communist invasion was thwarted, 21,940 Canadians had served under the blue flag of the United Nations. In those same years Canada had returned to the familiar fields of Europe with an extra-strength brigade of infantry and 12 fighter squadrons – our contribution to the N.A.T.O. watchdog force.

Lt.-Col. J. R. Stone, 2nd Battalion, P.P.C.L.I. checks maps before an attack.

Pte. Laurent Bourdeau, Le Royal 22e Régiment, makes a C-ration breakfast in a deep trench reminiscent of the Western Front in the Great War. The *Van Doos* held grimly to Hill 355 against heavy Chinese attacks. The fighting for "Little Gibraltar" showed that the Chinese were still tactically backward.

Face still blackened from the night patrol, wound in his leg awaiting attention, Pte. Morris Cantwell sits in the R.C.R. aid post.

Opposite In a "hot dog stand" over a Korean valley, a Canadian machine-gunner watches for any threat from the Communist side. One unusual foe caused many casualties: poison oak.

The many chores of the world's new cop

As the years of the Fifties and the Sixties proved that the Communists would seek total power by any means whereever they felt the West was most vulnerable, Canadians found themselves in tourist-poster countries – from the Vale of Kashmir to the Pyramids of Gizeh. They upheld, in strict impartiality, and at considerable cost, the high ideals of the United Nations. But, when we started to get brickbats instead of bouquets, Ottawa began to question the "policeman" policy.

Just how queer can a war get? At Khikimo, in the Kyrenian mountains of Cyprus, Canadian soldiers stand guard as a farmer gets in his barley. After three years of this stalemate between Greeks and Turks, the Canadians began to wonder when the "crisis" would end.

At right Keeping the peace in the Sinai desert, this Canadian jeep was blown up on the Egyptian side of the border with Israel. Two men died.

A Canadian jeep party patrols the walls of San'a, in the Arabian state of the Yemen, where Egyptian forces support rebels trying to overthrow the traditional regal rulers.

In the savage Congo, Lieut.-Col. Paul A. Mayer, of Ottawa, checks plans with his Swedish pilot for the rescue of hostage missionaries. Nuns were raped and murdered.

Since 1954, Canadian officers have been supervising the "truce" in Vietnam. When Communist North Vietnam infiltrated the South, it was a repetition of Korea but, this time, an enlarged United Nations did not support the *status quo*.

Rebuff in the Middle East: A time for sober reflection

On May 27, 1967, Egypt ordered the *immediate* withdrawal of the Canadians in the United Nations Emergency Force from the Middle East. Only the Canadians in the ten-nation peace-keeping force were affected by this peremptory demand and, when the Secretary-General acquiesced, the R.C.A.F. lifted the men in 21 flights in 48 hours. The Egyptians, armed to the teeth by the Russians, were once more threatening to sweep the Jews out of Israel. A week later, the desert was aflame again and the whole future of U.N. action under a cloud.

Like a scene in television's "Rat Patrol," armed jeeps of the Royal Canadian Signal Corps skid down a dune near the Gaza Strip in the Sinai desert. Each week they tested the emergency radio link-up with the Rafah base. When the Arab-Israeli war was resumed in 1967, 14 Indian members of the United Nations contingent were killed.

Opposite Wearing the blue berets that signify their United Nations status, tired Canadians return from their frustrating experience in the Middle East. People were asking: What's the use of a fire brigade that departs at the first sign of fire?

WEATHER
Cloudy and cool. Low tonight 50. High Tuesday 62. Mainly sunny and cool. Details Page 2.

THE TELEGRAM

50 PAGES
92ND YEAR

TORONTO, MONDAY, MAY 29, 1967

10 CENTS
TEL: 367-4500

1867 1967

'A LOSS OF FACE' FOR CANADA, SAYS DIEF

Nasser boots out our troops

Now the question is: What's next?

In the nation's 100th year – despite the preoccupation of press and television with a curious minority of youths, often with girly locks, who opt out of responsibility – more than 1,000 recruits a month were joining Canada's armed forces. The total enlistment, given in mid-year by Minister of Defence Paul Hellyer, was 105,972. The comparison with 1939, at the outbreak of the World War, could hardly be more dramatic: that year (when unemployment was rife), all three services together boasted 9,400 men.

With Canadians serving in so many exotic spots abroad, getting into uniform offered the adventurous an even better chance than ever before to "see the world." And the chances of getting hurt, looking at the averages over the past two decades, were higher on the Macdonald-Cartier Freeway. With Russia and America achieving something close to military balance, the possibility of full-scale C.B.R. warfare (Chemical, Biological, Radiological: the current jargon for Armageddon) seems increasingly remote.

In the mid-Sixties, Minister Hellyer raised more ire and controversy in the conservative world of the high brass than anyone since the unforgettable Sam Hughes. Hughes scorned the military establishment in 1914 and sent the battalions to France with prosaic numbers instead of the rolling tradition-tinged names beloved by the Militia regiments (example: 17th Duke of York's Royal Canadian Hussars); Hellyer went a giant step further and merged the Army, Navy and Air Force into the unified, one-uniform Canadian Armed Forces.

The individual serviceman finds his role basically unchanged under unification but the whole force is to be shaped into a unique inter-locking, inter-dependent instrument, no longer handicapped by jurisdictional frets or seniority wrangles, hopefully saved from the operation

of Parkinson's Law under which the administration and supply tail has grown unhealthily long in Canadian units at the expense of the fighting fist. The building of a highly trained Mobile Command, complete with its own supporting arms and its own jet transport, ready for service anywhere in the world, has led one fire-eating columnist (a winner of the Military Cross) to suggest a further renaming to "the Royal Canadian Commandos."

It remains a quirk of national attitude that many Canadians choose to believe they are a non-violent, unmilitary people. They are, indeed, slow to anger and rightly hesitant in the use of their now-considerable strength, but the events in this book (and it does not pretend to be a complete record) show that Canadians are, in fact, among the world's foremost fighting peoples. At times, it is difficult to suppress the thought that we have eagerly horned our way into just about any scrap that happened to be going.

The present absorption with United Nations' missions was put into its proper perspective by the Government during the debate on unification. It dismissed as "nonsensical" the suggestion that the Canadian forces were being converted into "a peace-keeping organization" with no capability beyond U.N. fire-brigade missions. The Defence Department will spend $270 millions a year for new equipment including gas-turbine destroyer escorts, more submarines, fighting helicopters, new attack aircraft, armoured vehicles, up-to-the-minute electronic communications equipment.

Whatever euphemisms might be conscripted to soothe the faint-hearted, Canada was constructing, for the very first time, a standing expeditionary force ready for armed intervention wherever the interests of the nation and its allies could best be served.

Inset Resisting unification of the Services to the last, some High Brass goes to a symbolic guillotine. The cartoonist has Defence Minister Hellyer at the reins of the tumbril.

Index

Victory portrait: Canada in the seats of power

Careful proof of Canada's assumption of high estate: Winston Churchill places General H. D. G. Crerar on his right and Lieut.-General G. G. Simonds on his left. Britain's Montgomery (in his famous two-badge beret) and Field Marshal Sir Alan Brooke complete the first row. The flanking officers are mostly Canadian brigadiers and colonels, including a future Chief of the General Staff (Brig. S. F. Clark, bareheaded *left).*

Acknowledgements

For their kind assistance with illustrations for this book, the Editors would particularly like to thank Major R. F. Wodehouse, Curator, War Collections, National Gallery of Canada, Mr. Edward Jablonski, author of *The Knighted Skies,* the Royal Canadian Military Institute in Toronto, and the staff of the Photo Establishment of the Department of Defence.

Note: The author wishes to thank Major John Newlands, archivist-historian of the Royal Canadian Military Institute, Toronto, for his advice and for checking the proofs. A large debt to the official historians of Canada's many military campaigns is also gratefully acknowledged. Any errors are, however, the exclusive property of the author.

Picture credits

Order of appearance in the text of pictures listed here is left to right, top to bottom. After the first recording, principal sources are credited under these abbreviatons:

Canadian Illustrated War News, CIWN

Chatelaine magazine, CM

Department of National Defence, DND

Edward Jablonski, EJ

Maclean's magazine, MM

Miller Services, MS

National Gallery of Canada, NG

Public Archives of Canada, PA

Royal Canadian Military Institute, Toronto, RCMI

Toronto Star Syndicate, TSS

Weekend magazine, WM

cover   Charles Comfort (detail), RCMI

1   NG courtesy *Weekend* magazine

2   Public Archives of Canada; Royal Canadian Military Institute; Department of National Defence

3   DND

4   RCMI

6-7   NG courtesy WM

8   The Burns Family Collection

9   "The Dawn of Majuba Day" by R. Caton Woodville, Corporation of the City of Toronto, courtesy RCMI

16-23   PA

24   *Canadian Illustrated War News* 1885, PA; *Illustrated London News* 1885, PA

25   CIWN 1885, PA; PA; CIWN, PA

26   PA; *Illustrated London News* 1885, *Maclean's* magazine

27   PA; PA; PA

28   RCMI

29   "Over the Top — Neuville Vitasse" by Alfred Bastien, NG

30   Photo by Dennis Colwell

34-35   PA

36-37   "The Battle of Frezenberg" RCMI

38   RCMI

38-39   PA

40   RCMI; PA; RCMI; RCMI

41-42   RCMI

42-43   RCMI, courtesy of *The Canadian* magazine

44   "The Taking of Vimy Ridge, Easter Monday, 1917" by Richard Jack, NG; PA; RCMI

45   "Vimy — The Canadians Capturing a German Trench" by W.B.Woolen, RCMI

46-49   RCMI

50-51   "Charge of Flowerdew's Squadron" by Alfred Munnings, NG

51   Drawing by F. M. L. Barthropp from *Canada's V.C.'s*

52-53   *The Standard* (Montreal), courtesy MM NG, WM

54-55   Toronto Star Syndicate; "The War Record" by Stanley Turner, NG TSS; "Women Operators" by G. A. Reid, NG

56   Culver Pictures; National Aviation Museum; RCAF, courtesy Edward Jablonski; PA

57   Jarrett Collection, courtesy EJ

58   RCAF, courtesy EJ; Jarrett Collection, courtesy EJ; Jarrett Collection, courtesy EJ

59   Painting by J. D. Carrick, RCMI

60   "General Sir Arthur Currie" by Sir William Orpen, NG, courtesy WM; "Lieut.-General Sir Sam Hughes" by Harrington Mann, NG

60-61

62   PA; RCMI

63   RCMI; RCMI; *Maple Leaf;* RCMI

64   RCMI; RCMI

65   RCMI; PA

66   RCMI

67-69   "Third Canadian Field Stationary Hospital at Doullens" by G. E. Moira, NG

70   "Patrol Dismissing in Camp" by E. J. Hughes, NG

71

76-77   DND

78   photo by Gilbert A. Milne

78-79   DND

80   "Oerlikon and Pom-Pom, HMCS Drumheller" by T. Wood, NG, courtesy RCMI; "South Side of St. Johns" by H. Beament, NG

81   "Atlantic Crossing" by Jack Nichols, NG

82   Miller Services; "Prison of War Camp Life in Hong Kong" by Lieut. A. V. Skvorzov, NG

83   DND; "Prison of War Camp Life in Hong Kong" by Lieut. A. V. Skvorzov, NG

84-85   "Landing at Dieppe" by Charles Comfort, NG courtesy RCMI

85   RCMI

86   *Chatelaine* magazine March 1944

87   National Film Board; TSS; "Gas Drill" by Molly Lamb, NG

88-89   CM, January 1944; CM, January 1944; *New World Illustrated,* June 1941; MM, January 1944; CM, January 1944; *New World Illustrated,* November 1941

90   MM; "Canteen Queue, Kiska" by Edward J. Hughes

91   Toronto Daily Star; TSS

92   "Canadian Tank in Sicily" by W. A. Ogilvie, NG

92-93   "Melfa River Crossings" by L. P. Harris, NG

94-95   DND

96   "Bomb Aimer, Battle of the Ruhr" by Carl Schaefer, NG; "Raid on San Guisto-Pisa" by P. A. Goranson, NG

97   "Zero Hour" by William Dring, NG

98   "Night Target, Germany" by Miller Brittain, NG

98-99   "R Day" by D. K. Anderson, NG courtesy RCMI

99   "Prang Bins" by Cloutier, NG

100   photo by Gilbert A. Milne

101   DND

102   "The Beach at Courseulles-sur-Mer" by Tom Wood, NG

103   DND

104   "Battle for Carpiquet Airfield" by Orville Fisher, NG

105   DND

106   DND; MS; DND

107   MS; DND; DND

108-110   DND

111   MS

112-113   DND

118   MS; DND; DND

119-122   DND

123   TSS   photo by Harold Barkley

124   cartoon by Franklin, TSS

126   DND

128   RCMI

This volume designed by Nick Milton
Printed and bound by Arnoldo Mondadori
Officine Grafiche Verona Italy
Typographer Cooper & Beatty Limited
Text and captions set in 9 point
Century and 7 point Helvetica respectively